FRESH BREAD IN THE MORNING
FROM YOUR BREAD MACHINE

FRESH BREAD IN THE MORNING FROM YOUR BREAD MACHINE

Annette Yates

RIGHT WAY

Constable & Robinson Ltd
3 The Lanchesters
162 Fulham Palace Road
London W6 9ER
www.right-way.co.uk
www.constablerobinson.com

First published in the UK 2003

This edition published by Right Way, an imprint of
Constable & Robinson Ltd, 2008

Copyright © Constable & Robinson, 2008

A copy of the British Library Cataloguing in Publication
Data is available from the British Library

ISBN: 978-0-7160-2154-4

Printed and bound in the EU

5 7 9 10 8 6

CONTENTS

Front cover photograph:
Michael Kay.

1

PUSH-BUTTON BREAD

Imagine waking up to the tantalising aroma of freshly baked bread filling your home! Next, picture yourself cutting thick slices of crusty bread to serve with cheese and a glass of wine. Or how about a buttery croissant to accompany your cappuccino, chewy bagels to serve with smoked salmon, or soft pitta bread for the children's packed lunch. Wishful thinking? Not when you have a bread machine. You can enjoy these simple pleasures each and every day – and all at the push of a button or two.

If you have ever felt nervous or intimidated by the thought of making your own bread, a bread machine is definitely for you. It transforms what can seem like a laborious, time-consuming and skilled process into a spectacularly easy affair. Until recently, I too was a reluctant maker of bread – on the one hand eager to experience the tactile and therapeutic pleasures it can bring; on the other hand desperately short of time. Now that I have a bread machine, we enjoy fresh bread every day and see little need to buy mass-produced loaves ever again.

When I was first asked to write this book, I confess to having questioned the wisdom of the idea. After all, bread machines are usually supplied with their own recipes – recipes that, in my opinion, produce bread that is far superior to any mass-produced loaf.

I put several machines to work on their basic recipes and soon discovered that many of them used what seemed like large amounts of yeast, salt, sugar, fat and dried milk powder. It made me wonder if they were really necessary to make a good loaf of bread, and what would happen if I reduced or omitted one or all of them. So I went back to basics, visiting flourmills and talking to expert bakers. They reminded me that traditional bread (in other words, bread made by hand with wholemeal, brown or unbleached white flour and baked in the oven) needs only flour, water and

7

small amounts of yeast and salt. My next step then was to take these four natural ingredients and put them in the bread machine to make a delicious loaf (the resulting recipe appears on page 40). I soon concluded that it mattered little to me if a loaf did not rise spectacularly high, look perfectly uniform or stay fresh for a long time. What I was seeking was freshly-baked well-risen bread (the sort that just begs to be eaten), made with minimum ingredients, having a lovely texture and a delicious flavour, and looking obviously home-made. This became the foundation for my section on every-day loaves.

As my baking progressed I learned that sugar, fat and milk powder can, and do, have roles to play in bread making, and explanations appear on pages 21 and 22. In my recipes, they feature to a small degree in the section on flavoured breads (page 55) and to a larger degree in hand-shaped doughs (page 75). In all instances however, they are included only when I believe their addition improves the finished result or when the recipe would not be traditional without them.

As well as plenty of recipes, I have put together all the information you need to get the best out of your bread machine. Within these pages you are likely to find answers to all your questions too, and much more besides.

In the writing of this book, I have sought the help of many. In particular, I would like to thank the following companies for supplying me with bread machines with which to test the recipes: Panasonic, Russell Hobbs, Breville, Morphy Richards, Prima and Hinari. My thanks also go to Shipton Mill, Doves Farm and Allinson for their advice on flours, and to Mike Hall, the miller at Y Felin, a twelfth century watermill at St Dogmaels in west Wales. Finally, I am most grateful to my publishers for their patience in allowing me plenty of extra time to test all the recipes several times over.

Enjoy using your bread machine and have fun trying out the recipes in this book. Happy button pushing!

Annette Yates

2

A BAKERY AT HOME

(OR ALL ABOUT BREAD MACHINES)

Using a bread machine is simple – you just add the ingredients to the bread pan, close the lid, choose your program and press the 'Start' button. Without any more effort from you, it will automatically mix, knead, prove and bake the bread.

WHAT TO LOOK FOR IN A BREAD MACHINE
A bread machine is best left on the kitchen worktop, ready for use at any time (mine is used at least once most days). So consider the space you have available and the shape and style that will best fit into your kitchen.

Bread machines are available in many shapes and sizes – in white, black or stainless steel – and with a variety of features. Though they all work in the same way, inevitably some are better than others. Of course, it's worth remembering that you are unlikely to be in a position where you can compare the results of one machine with another, so as long as YOUR machine produces bread that you and your family enjoy, that's all that matters.

A bread machine is basically an insulated box with a hinged lid. The main body contains the working parts, including the motor, the heating elements and the control panel. Inside, a removable non-stick bread pan (with a handle) locks into position. In the pan is a non-stick kneading blade that fits on to a rotating mounting shaft. Some larger models have two kneading blades, each fitted to its own mounting shaft.

The shape and size of the bread pan dictates the shape and size of the bread. When buying your first machine, it may be tempting to buy a small model but remember that small ones are unlikely to be able to make large loaves while larger machines can usually make small loaves. The most versatile machines are those that will make three sizes – small, medium and large.

The lid usually has an air vent to allow steam to escape. Sometimes a window is fitted in it, enabling you to view the bread as it cooks. In my experience, machines with a large window tend to produce bread with a slightly softer and paler top crust than those with a small or no window.

At the time this book is going to press, I have found that machines with the longer programs are the ones that consistently produce the best bread. Longer programs give the yeast plenty of time to do its work and make the bread rise. An added bonus is that the slower the bread rises, generally the better is its flavour. The best machines have programs that take 3-4 hours for white bread, 4-5 hours for wholewheat bread, 2-2½ hours for white dough and about 3 hours for wholewheat dough. Though these may seem long, remember, the bread machine is doing all the work while you get on with other things (just like a washing machine cleaning your clothes – imagine how much time and effort you would need to do it by hand). Bread machines with shorter programs can be good too – they usually require the addition of lukewarm liquids in order to speed up the rising process.

Most bread machines are supplied with a measuring cup and measuring spoons.

When choosing a bread machine for the first time, look for a well-written instruction book with enough basic, and not-so-basic, recipes to get you started. The best machines have a

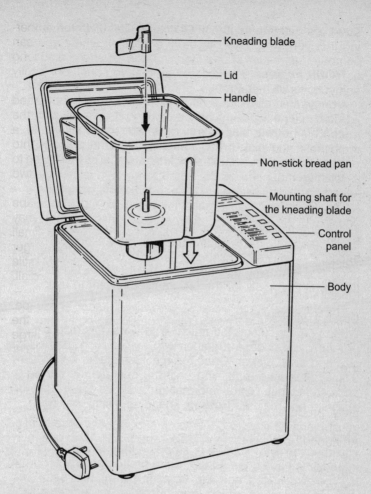

Kneading blade

Lid

Handle

Non-stick bread pan

Mounting shaft for
the kneading blade

Control
panel

Body

A typical bread machine.

good back-up service too, in case you need help and advice.

Power Failure

Good bread machines incorporate built-in safety devices that allow for a short break in power supply (if the machine is accidentally switched off or in the event of a brief power cut) as well as an automatic cut-out to stop the machine if the kneading blade is prevented from turning (by dough that is too dry and heavy for example).

CONTROLS

These are usually on a touch control panel on the top of the bread machine. Like controls on all new electrical appliances, they may take a short while to get used to, but you will soon find your way around them and become familiar with the correct symbols for the programs you want to use.

Display window

When you are setting the machine to work, this displays the program you choose together with extras such as the loaf size and crust colour. Once the machine starts, the window displays the time remaining until the operation is complete and, sometimes, extra information such as the stage the program has reached (resting, kneading, rising, baking).

Start/Stop

This function is for starting or stopping the machine once the ingredients have been added to the bread pan, the program has been selected and the timer (if using) has been set. When the bread machine is in operation an indicator light glows or flashes.

Menu buttons

These control the programs by choosing the type of bread or dough you are making, the size of loaf, crust colour and so on. Some have separate buttons for each function; others have one button that can be used to select a numbered program.

Size

Press this to choose the size loaf you wish to bake or (sometimes) the amount of dough you want to make. The choice varies with the model but, usually, the sizes are small, medium and large (450g/1 lb, 675g/1½ lb and 900g/2 lb) and refer to the size of the cooked loaf.

Crust colour
Most bread machines are set to cook a crust of 'medium' colour, unless you use this button to choose a lighter or darker crust. Ingredients such as sugar, eggs and cheese can cause the crust to darken quickly. If this happens the first time you make a recipe, this button allows you to adjust the colour next time. Similarly, if a loaf is too pale the first time you cook it, set the crust colour to a darker shade next time.

Delay timer
This is used to delay the cycle so that the bread machine switches on automatically and makes the bread in time to coincide with, perhaps, breakfast or your return home from work. The timer should not be used for recipes that include perishable ingredients, such as milk, yogurt, soft cheese, eggs, meat or fish.

PROGRAMS
The choice of programs differs slightly from manufacturer to manufacturer and model to model. Each will have been thoroughly tested using the manufacturer's own recipes, with kneading, rising and baking times to suit the sort of flour being used and the type of bread or dough required. When buying a bread machine, it's worth checking the programs and features and asking yourself which will be most useful to you. Here is a brief guide.

Baking Programs
These programs take the ingredients automatically through the normal bread-making process of mixing, kneading (pummelling and stretching), rising, knocking back (punching out the bubbles), kneading, rising and baking.

Basic White or Normal – the best program for loaves made with strong white, brown and soft grain flours.

Wholewheat – the best program for loaves made with strong wholemeal flour.

Rapid – shorter, and therefore faster, these programs are usually available for white or wholewheat loaves. Loaves made on these programs are likely to be smaller (and have a closer texture) than those cooked on full programs. Their keeping qualities are likely to be less too. In other words, these programs are fine if you need a fresh loaf in about one hour and plan to use it immediately.

Sandwich – for loaves with a softer crust and a fairly close texture, that are ideal for slicing to make sandwiches.

Dough Programs
These programs automatically mix the ingredients, knead (pummel and stretch) the dough and allow it to rise in ideal conditions. Then it is removed from the bread machine, knocked back (has the gas bubbles punched out of it) and kneaded briefly (worked by pressing and stretching) before being shaped by hand, allowed to prove (rise for a second time) and then baked conventionally in a hot oven.

White – for making dough with white, brown and soft grain flours.

Wholewheat – for making dough with wholemeal flour.

Pizza – a shorter program for making dough that is ideal for making flatbreads such as pizza bases, pitta bread and focaccia.

ADDITIONAL FEATURES
Add extra ingredient 'beep' or **raisin 'beep'** – a really useful feature that lets you know the right time in the cycle to add extra ingredients such as nuts and dried fruit.

Raisin/Nut dispenser – automatically adds small amounts of additional ingredients to the dough at the correct stage during the cycle. This is fine for dry foods (such as nuts and seeds) but ingredients that are likely to stick in the dispenser (chopped raw or dried fruits, grated cheese and chocolate) need to be added by hand.

Keep-warm facility – keeps the bread warm for up to an hour after it is baked.

Power alert – tells you that there has been a break in the power supply.

Expert mode – allows you to program each stage in the procedure to suit your individual requirements.

Extended bake or **extra bake** facility – enables you to add extra baking time to the basic programs.

Cake or **bake program** – for baking only (some models mix and bake); useful for cakes and tea breads.

French program – a longer program that makes a loaf with a crust that is crisp and a texture that is open.

Italian program – for Italian-style loaves that often contain oil as an ingredient.

Gluten-free program – specifically designed to mix, rise and bake gluten-free bread mixes.

Fan-assisted baking – sometimes built in to bread machines that have a large viewing window.

Jam program – for making small amounts of jam.

Bagel/roll rack – a stand or rack that is specially designed to hold bagels or rolls in the bread machine during baking.

3

WHAT MAKES A LOAF OF BREAD?

Wheat Flour

The type of bread made depends on the sort of flour used. In a bread machine, it is important to use a high proportion of 'strong' or 'bread' flour since it contains plenty of proteins that, when mixed with water, develop gluten. It is this gluten that makes the dough elastic and allows it to stretch and rise, while trapping in the bubbles of gas produced by the yeast.

Bread flour is made by milling the kernels of hard wheat. Most flour is mass-produced using steel rollers; the rest is made traditionally by crushing the wheat between millstones (and is called 'stoneground' flour). There are three main parts to the wheat kernel – the bran or husk (the tough outer coating), the germ or the seed, and the endosperm (the inner bit that contains the starch and the protein).

Choose flour that is labelled 'strong', 'bread', 'Canadian', 'extra strong' or 'for bread machines'. I like to use organic varieties whenever possible. When I can grab the opportunity, I buy direct from the numerous small flourmills that are dotted all round the country producing wonderfully distinctive flours.

Store it in a cool, dry and dark place that has some ventilation.

Use it by the correct date (see the best-before or use-by date on the packaging).

Avoid mixing new flour with old stock.

Dispose immediately of any flour that does not smell quite right or that develops signs of flour mites or weevils.

Wholemeal or wholewheat flour is made by grinding the entire wheat kernel, with nothing removed. It has a coarse consistency and bread made entirely with wholemeal flour has a robust texture and a full flavour. The dough rises more slowly than that made with white flour and the finished loaves are generally smaller and heavier than white ones.

Brown flour (sometimes called wheatmeal) has had 10-20 per cent of the wheat germ and some of the bran removed. As a result, it produces bread that is lighter than wholemeal but with a coarser texture and a fuller flavour than white.

Strong white or **bread flour** is made from hard wheat that has had the bran and germ removed. The endosperm has been ground to a fine white flour that produces a light white loaf with a smooth shape. Today's strong bread flours remain unbleached and can appear slightly grey – to my mind this is preferable to bleaching.

Canadian bread flour and **extra strong bread flour** generally have a slightly higher percentage of protein than normal strong white or bread flour. They give particularly good results in bread machines.

Granary-style or **malted grain flour** usually contains a mixture of wholemeal, strong white and rye flours with the addition of soft, malted wheat grain (the actual combination varies slightly between brands). Bread made with this flour is quite light with an interesting texture and a sweetish, nutty flavour.

Other Flours
Semolina flour is milled from the endosperm of durum wheat (one of the hardest wheat types) and is available coarse or fine. Though semolina flour produces a high proportion of gluten, it produces dough that is tough. This makes it ideal for pasta but when making bread it is best used in small quantities in combination with other wheat flours. (Try using it in place of cornmeal in the recipe on page 45.)

Spelt flour is a high-protein flour that is made from an ancient grain that is related to wheat. It's best combined with other flours (see recipe on page 44).

Rye flour is a low-gluten flour that is produced from milled grains of rye grass. On its own it produces a heavy, dark dough that is difficult to work with. Mixed with wheat flours, it gives the bread a distinctive flavour (see recipe on page 43).

Cornmeal or **maize flour** is a fine yellow flour that is milled from dried kernels of corn. Because it is gluten-free it cannot be used on its own in the bread machine, but mixed with white bread flour it adds colour, texture and a sweet flavour. Polenta is a slightly coarser version of cornmeal (see recipe on page 45).

Buckwheat flour is ground from the seeds of a herb that is native to Russia. It is greyish-brown in colour and adds an assertive, slightly bitter flavour. It is gluten-free and is often used in pancakes. In the bread machine it should be mixed in small amounts with wheat flours (see recipe on page 46).

Oat flour is gluten-free and is made by grinding oats from which the outer husk has been removed. This flour is not easy to obtain, so try using oatmeal or rolled oats (see recipe on page 48) or grind your own in a food processor.

Millet flour is a low-gluten flour made from ground millet seeds. Use it in very small quantities with other wheat flours to add texture.

Barley flour or barley meal is another low-gluten flour. Made from barley seeds that have had their bran removed (pearl barley), it has a distinctive 'earthy' flavour. Use it in small amounts with white bread flour.

Rice flour or ground rice is milled from grains of rice and is available brown or white. It is gluten-free, so use a small amount with white bread flour to add a little sweetness and a slightly chewy texture to your bread.

Soy flour is made by grinding soybeans to a fine powder. Unlike the other flours, it contains a high proportion of protein and hardly any starch. Used in very small quantities with other bread flours, it will increase the protein content of the bread while adding a mild flavour.

'Gluten-free' flour. As this book goes to press, there is at least one company (Doves Farm) producing a gluten-free bread flour that is suitable for bread machines. It contains a special blend of non-wheat flours (such as rice, potato and tapioca) and a natural (xanthan) gum. Detailed instructions for making loaves in a bread machine (or by hand) are printed on the packet. The BASIC WHITE program is usually suitable.

Yeast

Yeast is used to leaven bread dough – in other words, it is what makes bread rise.

So what is yeast? It is a microscopic living organism that, in the right conditions (moist and warm), grows by converting its food (sugar and starch) into gas (carbon dioxide) and alcohol. The moisture is supplied by the liquid in the recipe, while the gentle warmth is controlled automatically by the bread machine. Sugar and starch are supplied by the flour and it is the carbon dioxide and the bubbles it creates that make the bread dough rise, while the alcohol evaporates during baking.

The most convenient type of yeast (and indeed the one that is recommended for all bread machines) is dried and packed in sachets or small packets, ready to put straight into the bread machine together with the other ingredients. It does not need to be dissolved in liquid first. Look for labels marked 'Easybake', 'Easy Blend', 'Quick' or 'Fast Action' – these are the ones to use.

Manufacturers of bread machines do not recommend fresh yeast (sold in blocks and can be difficult to obtain anyway) or ordinary 'active' dried yeast (sold in small resealable cans). These need to be dissolved in water before use and are difficult to handle in bread machines.

How much yeast you use will depend on your bread machine and on the ingredients in the recipe. Generally, I have found that 1 tsp per 500g/1 lb 2 oz is a good guide. Once the yeast packet has been opened, use it fairly promptly – check the label for guidance.

Salt

As well as adding flavour to bread, salt also has vital roles to play.

Salt slows down the growth of yeast and adding a small amount to the bread mixture helps prevent the yeast from growing so much that the dough reaches the lid of the bread machine and collapses. However, too much salt will prevent the yeast growing at all and the result is a small, heavy loaf.

Adding a little salt also helps to strengthen the gluten, helping the dough to stretch and allowing the bread to rise and hold its shape. Too much will toughen the gluten, severely prevent stretching and result in a dense loaf.

The recipes in this book use finely ground sea salt, a pure salt that is produced by evaporating seawater – a costly process which is reflected in the price. I think it's worth it but you can of course use finely ground rock salt or ordinary table salt. Salt substitutes are not suitable.

How much salt to use? A good guide is ½-1¼ tsp per 500g/1 lb 2 oz flour.

When adding salt to the bread machine, make sure it is kept away from the yeast – particularly if you are using the delay timer.

Liquid

Liquid is needed to bind all the ingredients together into dough, to rehydrate the dried yeast and to allow the yeast to grow. The temperature of that liquid will be dictated by your bread machine and the program you choose. Your instruction book will tell you whether to add the liquid cold, at room temperature or lukewarm.

The quantity of liquid required will depend on the recipe. Too little and the bread will not mix or rise well; too much and the dough is likely to collapse (see page 123).

Water is the usual ingredient and it gives the bread a crisp crust and a light, slightly stretchy crumb. I am lucky enough to live in an area that supplies soft, fresh-tasting water, which I am happy to use in my bread machine. Tap water that is hard or heavily treated with chlorine and fluoride can slow down the growth of yeast. If this is the case in your area (or simply if you prefer), you may like to use filtered water or bottled still spring water.

Milk produces a softer, browner crust. Because it contains protein and (in the case of full and semi-skimmed) fat, it makes a crumb that is tender and slightly rich. The sugars in milk help to feed the yeast, encouraging it to grow. Milk should not be used on a delayed program – it is likely to turn sour during several hours sitting around in the bread machine. Instead, use milk powder, making sure that it cannot come into contact with the water until the program starts.

Buttermilk and **yogurt** add a tangy, slightly acidic flavour to bread and give it a moist, tender crumb (as in Half-and-Half with Buttermilk on page 54 and Spiced Cranberry Bread on page 69).

Fruit juices add a slight sweetness and a delicate fruity flavour to the bread dough (as in Minted Bread on page 67). The fruit sugar helps the yeast to grow.

Beer, ale and cider can add interesting flavours and the sugars in them help the yeast to grow. Dark beers add colour too and, I think, make stunning loaves that are full of character (see Porter Bread on page 70).

Eggs (see page 23) should be included when calculating the liquid in a recipe.

Sugar
The yeast available for bread machines today (see above) does not need sugar in order to work. However, the addition of a small amount can provide extra food for the yeast,

enabling it to grow faster and making a bread that is moist and with good keeping qualities.

As you will see, many of the basic bread recipes in this book contain little or no added sugar. For me, one of the pleasures of having a bread machine is to be able to eat bread on the day it is made, so there is little point in adding unnecessary ingredients to a bread that is delicious just as it is. When I do want to add sugar, I like to use natural products like malt extract (my favourite), honey and maple syrup; unrefined brown sugars (such as muscovado); molasses and golden granulated or golden caster sugar. Of course, you can also use white sugars (granulated and caster), golden syrup and treacle. Artificial sweeteners are not suitable for use in the bread machine.

A large quantity of sugar will slow down the growth of the yeast. In bread machines, this means that rich doughs (such as Barm Brack on page 96) can be mixed on a DOUGH program, after which they will then need to be removed from the bread machine and left to rise slowly before baking in the oven.

Fat (oils, margarine, butter)
The addition of a small amount of fat enriches bread, making it moist and tender. It can also improve its flavour and extend its keeping qualities.

In my basic recipes in this book, you will see that I rarely use fat – this is because I think that bread can be delicious with the minimum of ingredients. However, when I think the result is improved by the addition of a small amount of fat, then I have included it. You will also find plenty of recipes for breads and rich doughs that would not be authentic without the addition of some fat (such as Focaccia on page 86 and Kugelhopf on page 120).

When I do add fat to a bread recipe, I usually prefer to use the oils that are considered healthy (such as olive and sunflower) and keep the hard fats (like butter, margarine and lard) for recipes where flavour or authenticity (or indeed both) is important. I never use reduced-fat spreads, preferring to use a small amount of olive or sunflower oil instead of adding the extra water and other ingredients that these products contain. When you want a loaf to keep fresh for a few days it is a good idea to add 1-2 tbsp oil or 15-25g/½-1 oz butter per 500g/1 lb 2 oz flour.

Eggs are used to make breads richer with a soft, tender texture and good keeping qualities. They also add colour, flavour and nutrients (protein and fat in particular). Because eggs contain a high proportion of water, they should be counted as part of the liquid when measuring out ingredients. Bread recipes that contain eggs are not suitable for delayed programs.

Vitamin C or Ascorbic Acid

This is used as a 'bread improver' by helping the yeast to grow in a short time and thus improving the volume of the finished loaf. You have probably noticed its inclusion in some white bread flours and in 'Easybake', 'Easy Blend', 'Quick' and 'Fast Action' yeast.

There is generally no need to add extra vitamin C to the bread machine, though it does help to give a better volume to wholemeal loaves (see page 51). Vitamin C (or ascorbic acid) can be bought from your local pharmacy, where you will need to explain that you will be using it for bread making. Alternatively, you could use fresh lemon juice, which naturally contains vitamin C – try using 2 tsp per 500g/1 lb 2 oz flour.

Other Ingredients

Wheat bran is the tough, outer husk that is removed from wheat grain during the milling process. Use it to add fibre, texture and flavour to your bread, but add a little only – no more that 4 tbsp per 500g/1 lb 2 oz flour – or it will make a loaf that is small and dense. Alternatively, it can be sprinkled on top of oven-baked breads.

Wheatgerm is the seed of the wheat kernel. It is present in wholemeal flour and, in lesser quantity, in brown flour. If you want to add it to your bread (to add texture, flavour or nutritional value), use it in small amounts only, like wheat bran, above.

Oat bran, the outer husk of oat kernels, is a valuable, soluble source of fibre. Use it like wheat bran, above.

Rolled or porridge oats have had the husks removed before being rolled into flakes. They add flavour, moisture and a lovely texture to bread (see page 48 for one of my favourite loaves).

Seeds give a lovely texture and flavour to bread. Pumpkin, sunflower, sesame, poppy and linseeds are my favourites. It's best to use a small quantity only because they tend to cut into the structure of the bread to make it slightly dense (the recipes on pages 58 and 59 will give you a guide). They should be added to the bread dough after the first mixing, kneading and rising – a beeping signal on the bread machine indicates that it is time to add them, or some machines have a dispenser which will add them automatically at the appropriate stage in the bread-making cycle (see pages 14 and 26). Seeds are good to use as toppings on oven-baked breads too.

Nuts such as walnuts, pecans, almonds, pistachios, hazelnuts and pine nuts make lovely additions to bread. Use them chopped, just as they are or lightly toasted. Like seeds (see above) use them in small quantities (see pages 60, 68 and 73 for a guide) only and add them at the appropriate stage in the bread-making cycle.

Dried fruits add moisture, flavour, colour and texture to breads. They are best added at the beeping signal. For loaves that are cooked in the bread machine, use small quantities only (see pages 57 and 69). If you want to add a high proportion of fruit, it's best to use a DOUGH program then work in extra fruit by hand before rising and baking it in the oven (like Chelsea Buns on page 103 and Stollen on page 106).

Dried herbs and spices can be used to give wonderful flavours to bread. Add them with the ingredients at the start of the program (as in Sage and Onion Loaf on page 66) or sprinkle them over the top of oven-baked breads (such as Focaccia on page 86).

Fresh herbs give a wonderful, fresh flavour and colour to bread. Try Minted Bread on page 67.

4

PRESSING BUTTONS

It's time to make a loaf of bread! You will of course need to follow the instructions that accompany your particular bread machine, but here is the basic method.

A FRESH LOAF OF BREAD IN FIVE EASY STEPS

1. **Measure the ingredients and add them to the bread pan.**
    Remove the bread pan from the machine before adding the ingredients (otherwise it is easy to spill them on to the heating elements where they will burn).

    The kneading blade should be in position (on its mounting shaft) before adding the ingredients.

    It is important to measure the ingredients accurately, using weighing scales and the measuring cups and spoons that come with your bread machine.

Add the ingredients to the pan in the correct order for your particular machine (follow the manufacturer's instructions).

2. Fit the bread pan into the bread machine and close the lid.
It should be surely locked into position with the handle folded down.

3. Select the appropriate program.
At the risk of being obvious, you will of course need to switch on the bread machine at the mains first!

Select the appropriate loaf size and crust colour.

When appropriate, set the delay timer too.

4. Press start.
The bread machine begins its cycle of mixing, kneading, rising and baking, alerting you (with a beeping sound) when it is time to add extra ingredients such as seeds or nuts.

At the end of the program a beeping signal will announce when the program has finished and the bread is cooked.

5. Turn the loaf out on to a wire rack and leave to cool.
Most bread machines will keep the cooked loaf warm for up to one hour. However, once the program has finished, it is better to turn the loaf out as soon as possible.

Use oven gloves to open the lid and remove the bread pan from the machine.

Turn the pan upside down and shake it several times until the loaf is released.

You may need to remove the kneading blade from the bread – use a heat-resistant utensil that will not scratch the non-stick surface, such as a wooden spatula or spoon.

Turn the loaf the right way up and leave to cool for at least 30 minutes (and preferably longer) before slicing.

Storing bread

Don't expect homemade bread to keep as long as commercially made varieties. In our house, freshly cooked bread is unlikely to last long anyway so, once it has cooled completely, I store it in a bread bin in the kitchen.

Experts maintain that the best way to store bread is to wrap it tightly in foil or seal it in a plastic bag and keep it at room temperature. Always resist the temptation to refrigerate bread because staling is at its most rapid in typical refrigerator temperatures.

If you really need to keep bread for longer than a day or two, the best way is to freeze it. With the exception of really crusty loaves, most fresh bread can be frozen for about four weeks wrapped and sealed in freezer bags. When you want to eat it, allow the bread to thaw (still in its bag) at room temperature or defrost it on a very low power in the microwave. If you use only small amounts of bread, it is a good idea to slice bread before freezing and take it out a few pieces at a time.

5

MAKE THE MOST OF YOUR BREAD MACHINE

For best results, follow the operating and care instructions that are provided with your bread machine. (An obvious statement, I know, but important nonetheless.)

Good results rely on good quality ingredients. The quality of the ingredients and their temperature will influence results. Flour, for example, can be affected by many things – crop, seasons, milling and storage conditions to name just some (see page 17), and yeast that is stale is unlikely to make good bread.

The starting temperature of the ingredients can affect results too, particularly if your bread machine does not have an initial rest or warming period at the start of the program. Do check with your instruction book for the ideal temperature of liquid ingredients in particular.

The weather and the room conditions are also likely to have an effect. In particular, keep the bread machine away from direct sunlight and draughts.

It is important to measure all ingredients accurately, using the spoons and cups provided with your bread machine and making sure that spoon measures (for yeast in particular) are level.

Always add the ingredients to the bread pan in the correct order for your particular machine.

When including perishable ingredients, such as milk or eggs, always start the program immediately. In other words, don't use the delay timer.

During mixing, if you need to scrape pieces of dough down from the sides of the bread pan, use a flexible spatula or a tool that will not scratch the non-stick lining.

The type and proportion of ingredients will affect the results of breads baked in the bread machine. Doughs containing wholemeal flour, extra ingredients (fruit, nuts, cheese and so on) or high proportions of fat, sugar or eggs are likely to rise more slowly than ordinary white, brown or granary bread. Doughs with a high fat (cheese, eggs, oil, butter) or sugar content are likely to brown quickly, so the first time you cook such a recipe, select the light crust setting.

Remove the loaf from the bread machine as soon as possible after baking. Although your machine probably has a 'keep warm' facility, the bread will not benefit from staying in it for long.

Always remember that bread machines differ from make to make and model to model. As with most kitchen appliances, you will soon get the feel of your bread machine and become confident in adjusting ingredients and recipes to suit it.

Wholemeal or Wholewheat?
Though these descriptions are often interchangeable, in this book, 'wholemeal' is used to describe flour while 'wholewheat' is the bread machine program used for recipes containing wholemeal flour.

ADAPTING RECIPES FOR YOUR BREAD MACHINE
Here are some hints and tips for those occasions when you spot a bread recipe in a book or magazine and wonder if is suitable for making in the bread machine. You will find the notes on pages 13, 16 and 122 helpful too.

- Check with a similar recipe in this book or your manufacturer's book and be guided by the amounts and
proportion of ingredients. Use the quantity of flour as
your main guide. Take care not to overload the bread
machine by exceeding the maximum recommended
quantity of flour.

- Instead of fresh yeast or ordinary dried yeast, use types
labelled 'Easybake', 'Easy Blend', 'Quick' or 'Fast
Action' (see page 19).

- If a recipe contains 100 per cent wholemeal flour, it's a
good idea to replace half of it with strong white bread
flour.

- Small amounts of butter can generally be replaced with
oil (and vice versa). There is no need to melt butter, just
cut it up into small pieces before adding it to the bread
pan.

- Remember to add the ingredients to the bread pan in
the correct order for your machine, keeping the yeast
away from the liquid and salt.

- Recipes that contain perishable ingredients (like milk
and eggs) should not be used with the delay timer.

- Choose a program to suit the type of flour. Recipes
containing entirely white or brown flour are generally
made on the BASIC WHITE program, while wholemeal
flours need the BASIC WHOLEWHEAT program. With
granary-style flours, bread machine manufacturers differ in their recommendations, so always be guided by
your instruction book.

- Select the size of loaf that most closely matches the
quantity of ingredients (use the flour as your main guide
and check with your instruction book). The recipes in this
book generally make medium or 675g (1½ lb) loaves.

- The first time you make a recipe in the bread machine, it
is a good idea to check the mixing process during the
early stages. This provides the opportunity to adjust the
consistency by adding a little extra water (if the mixture is

too dry) or flour (if it is too wet). The aim is to make a soft, smooth (not sticky) dough that gathers into a ball. A mixture that is too dry or heavy may overload the motor by making it work too hard; a mixture that is too wet will not rise well. Add any extra flour or water in small spoonfuls until the correct consistency is reached.

- Keeping an eye on the cycle at regular intervals (and making notes) will help you to decide how to adjust the recipe in future.

- If you are unsure whether a recipe is suitable and do not want to risk failure, make the dough in the bread machine (using a DOUGH program) then shape it by hand and leave it to rise before baking in the oven. The same applies if you find that a recipe mixes, kneads and rises well in the bread machine but you are disappointed with the baked loaf.

- Don't even attempt to cook doughs that are rich in fat, sugar, eggs or fruit in the bread machine. Instead, use a DOUGH cycle then shape the dough by hand, leave it to rise and bake in the oven.

BREAD MIXES

Ready-prepared bread mixes (where the yeast is mixed in with the other ingredients) can be put into a bread machine and are usually cooked on the RAPID programs. Follow the instructions given by the manufacturers of the bread machine and the bread mix.

In bread mixes where the yeast is supplied in a separate sachet, select a program that suits the type of flour mix. For example, white and brown mixes should cook well on BASIC WHITE programs, while wholemeal flour would be better on a (longer) WHOLEWHEAT program.

Gluten-free bread mixes

Unless your bread machine has a special program for gluten-free mixes, it is best to use a RAPID WHITE program. On occasions when I have used these mixes, best results have been obtained by making up the mixture before adding it to the bread machine.

(Note: please see page 19 for information on gluten-free flour.)

6

FINISHING TOUCHES

PREPARING DOUGH (MADE IN THE BREAD MACHINE) FOR OVEN COOKING

For me, one of the joys of having a bread machine is to be able to make dough that I can quickly shape by hand into loaves, flatbreads, rolls and so on, then leave to rise before baking in a hot oven. The machine saves me time and hard work by doing the initial mixing, kneading, resting and rising. Consequently, you will find a whole chapter devoted to my favourite dough recipes that begins on page 75.

Here are some guidelines for working with dough. (The notes also provide a rough description of what happens automatically in the bread machine during the latter stages of a normal baking program.)

● When your chosen dough program has finished (a series of beeps will sound to let you know), lift the bread pan out of the machine and tip the dough, easing it out with your hand, on to a lightly floured surface.

- **Knock back** the dough by gently punching out the gas bubbles. You will already feel it change from a soft, light and aerated mixture to one that is easier to handle.

- **Knead** the dough lightly by pressing it down and pushing away from you, then folding it in half and repeating the process. Do this two or three times only, using the lightly floured surface to help you, until the dough feels satiny smooth and elastic. Use only enough flour to prevent sticking and don't overwork the dough by kneading it too much.

  Don't be too worried about technique – the idea is simply to press and stretch the dough, developing the gluten (see page 16) and dividing up the pockets of air and gas to achieve an even texture in the finished bread. Sometimes, a coarse texture (or a combination of dense crumb with large pockets) is desirable (as in Italian-style bread on page 92). Whatever the result, it will simply highlight the fact that the bread is home-made and therefore a real treat.

- **Rest** the dough for 5-10 minutes, if time allows, before shaping. This allows the dough to relax and become easier to handle.

- **Shape** the dough into loaves or rolls by gently pressing and folding it into your desired shape(s). This is where you can really have fun making new and interesting shapes – children particularly love to make weird shapes, flowers and animals.

  If the dough becomes tight and difficult to handle, just let it rest (relax) for a minute or two before continuing.

  If you plan to bake the bread in a loaf tin, first press and fold it into the correct shape, then put it into the greased tin and press down lightly with your knuckles, gently pushing the dough into the corners of the tin.

  Whatever the shape, for loaves or rolls, grease the baking sheet first and always make sure that the top surface of the dough is smooth and that all seams are tucked away underneath.

- For most dough, the next stage is to leave it to **prove (or rise)** and achieve its final shape and texture before baking.

Covering the dough loosely during rising keeps it clean and prevents moisture loss and a crust forming on the dough. Either use lightly oiled film (with the oiled side against the dough) or a clean tea towel.

Most shapes need to almost double in size, though some flatbreads, such as pitta (page 89) and naan (page 90), are hardly allowed to rise at all. The time this takes will depend on the dough mixture and its shape and size, and the temperature of the room. Experts say that the ideal temperature is about 27-32°C/80-90°F. Don't be disheartened if it seems to take a long time – dough that is allowed to rise slowly is likely to have a superior flavour. It is, however, important that the room is free from draughts.

To check that the dough is ready for baking, press it lightly with your fingertip. It should feel spongy and spring back into shape. Dough that is allowed to rise for too long tends to collapse slightly when touched or when it goes into the heat of the oven.

Cutting into the top surface of loaves or rolls gives them a decorative finish. This should be done with a very sharp knife either before or after the final rising. Cuts or slashes that are made after rising need to be done very carefully in order to prevent the dough from collapsing.

- **Bake** the bread in a hot oven (it can be preheated while the dough is proving). The temperature of the oven is dictated by the type of bread being cooked and its shape and size. See the recipes for guidance.

When the risen dough is put into the hot oven, it rises rapidly for a short, final time (this is appropriately called 'oven spring') before the yeast is killed and the dough sets. Dough that is over-proved tends to collapse at this stage because the gas pockets burst before the dough has had a chance to solidify. During the remainder of the cooking time, the centre of the dough cooks through while the outside crust crisps up and turns an attractive brown.

A steamy atmosphere (created by putting a shallow container of water in the bottom of the oven) helps to produce a crisp crust on the bread.

Check that the bread is cooked by tapping the bottom of the loaf or roll. It should sound hollow. If not, return it to the oven (preferably upside down) for a little longer.

- Leave the bread to **cool**. Transfer the hot bread to a wire rack and allow it to cool for at least 30 minutes (preferably longer for large loaves) before cutting – to allow the temperature and pressure to even out. I know that the temptation to eat bread hot out of the oven is difficult to resist but, believe me, it will be almost impossible to cut and is likely to collapse into a dense, heavy mess. So be patient!

GLAZES AND OTHER TOPPINGS

Glazes and/or toppings can transform simple plain dough into something stunning by adding colour, flavour and texture.

For loaves that are cooked in the bread machine, brush on the glaze or add the topping just before, or as soon as, baking begins. Be quick (so you lose as little heat from the machine as possible) and be gentle so as not to knock the gas out of the dough. Keep glazes and toppings that are likely to burn (sugar or cheese for example) away from the sides of the bread pan.

Rolls and other breads that are baked in the oven can be glazed before or during cooking.

Some glazes, as you will see below, are best added after baking, while the bread is still warm.

Glazes

Milk – brushed over loaves or rolls before baking, it gives a golden crust that is fairly soft. It also serves as an adhesive, helping toppings like grains and seeds to stick to the surface during and after baking.

Egg – egg white, beaten with a little water and brushed on before baking, gives a pale gold, shiny crust; egg yolk mixed with water or milk gives a rich golden, shiny crust. Alternatively, use the whole egg, beaten with a little water. Like milk, it can be used as a bonding agent for seeds and grains.

Salted water – brush the uncooked dough with lightly salted water for a crisp crust with a slight shine.

Olive oil – frequently used on French- and Italian-style breads before or/and after baking. Olive oil will add its own individual flavour and give the bread a moist texture (see

Focaccia, page 86). Breads with oil are particularly suitable for reheating.

Butter – melted and brushed on to dough before baking, it produces a soft, golden brown crust with a rich flavour. Brushed over cooked bread, butter makes the crust soft and extends the keeping qualities of the loaf. A good example is Stollen on page 106.

Honey – warmed and brushed over cooked breads, it adds a distinctive flavour and makes the crust deliciously sticky and soft.

Malt extract – use it like honey (above). I love its rich flavour, though it may need diluting to taste.

Sugar (molasses, muscovado or golden) – dissolve a little in warm water or milk and brush on to freshly baked bread to give a lovely shine and a soft crust, as in Hot Cross Buns on page 98. Alternatively, blend some icing sugar with liquid (water, fruit juice, brandy) to make a thin icing and drizzle or brush over the top of warm breads.

Jams and marmalades – heat with a little liquid and brush over the top of freshly baked breads.

Toppings
Flour – for a rustic finish, dust the risen dough with a little flour of your choice just before baking.

Wheat bran, oat bran and rolled oats – just before baking, lightly brush the risen dough with milk or egg and sprinkle with bran or oats.

Cornmeal or polenta – lightly brush the dough with water and sprinkle it over.

Salt – for a crunchy, salty crust, sprinkle with coarse sea salt after brushing with oil or egg.

Seeds – give the top crust a crunchy texture by glazing the dough then sprinkling with seeds such as caraway, cumin, mustard, poppy, pumpkin, sesame or sunflower seeds (or a mixture). Hand-shaped doughs can be rolled in seeds before the final rising.

Herbs – brush the risen dough with oil (I use olive) and sprinkle with herb leaves such as oregano, rosemary or thyme.

Spices – add flavour and colour by sprinkling spices, such as ground cumin, coriander, paprika, chilli or mixed spice, over the risen dough before baking.

Cheese – grated cheese sprinkled over before baking makes the crust chewy and very tasty.

Sugar – sift icing sugar over the top of baked and cooled rolls such as Devonshire Splits (page 101).

Nuts – flaked, chopped or whole, can be sprinkled on top of a sweet glaze.

7

BREAD WINNERS

The recipe section is divided into everyday loaves and flavoured breads that are made entirely in the bread machine, and hand-shaped, oven-baked doughs. I hope you enjoy them as much as I do.

Measurements
Metric and imperial measurements are given in the recipes but please be aware that they are not always exact conversions. It's best to use one type of measurement at a time (either metric or imperial and not a mixture of the two). This is because some figures have been rounded up or down in order to achieve the correct proportions and get the best results.

And don't forget; always use the measuring spoons and cups that are supplied with your bread machine. All spoon measurements are level.

STAFF OF LIFE

(OR EVERYDAY LOAVES)

In life before bread machines, a homemade loaf fresh out of the oven for breakfast would have been but a dream for most of us. A bread machine makes it possible to have fresh bread on a daily basis – bread that is made with exactly the ingredients you choose. Since most of us tend to eat some bread every day, it's good to know what's going into it and that we are in control. If, like me, you want to improve your diet to include more natural and fresh foods with fewer non-essential ingredients, the recipes in this section will help. Whenever possible, they are made with basic ingredients and the minimum of yeast, salt, sugar and fat. Most of them are free from dairy products such as milk too.

Should you decide to adjust the ingredient quantities, the notes on pages 16-24 will be helpful.

Everyday White Loaf

This is the bread that I remember as a child, made with nothing but flour, yeast, salt and water – its golden, splintering crust surrounding the light and slightly stretchy inside. This loaf is impossible to slice warm and I have to resist the temptation simply to tear it apart and eat the lot, with or without butter!

1 tsp Easybake yeast
500g/1 lb 2 oz strong white bread flour
1¼ tsp fine sea salt
350ml/12 fl oz water

1. Put the ingredients into the bread pan in the correct order for your machine.

2. Fit the pan into the bread machine and close the lid.

3. Select the BASIC WHITE setting, MEDIUM CRUST and the appropriate SIZE. Press Start.

4. When the program has finished, lift the bread pan out of the machine, turn the bread out on to a wire rack and leave to cool completely.

Light White with Honey

A bread with a crisp crust, light texture and delicate flavour – a spoonful of good-quality runny honey is the only addition to the basic ingredients.

1 tsp Easybake yeast
500g/1 lb 2 oz strong white bread flour
1¼ tsp fine sea salt
1 tbsp clear honey
350ml/12 fl oz water

1. Put the ingredients into the bread pan in the correct order for your machine.

2. Fit the pan into the bread machine and close the lid.

3. Select the BASIC WHITE setting, MEDIUM CRUST and the appropriate SIZE. Press Start.

4. When the program has finished, lift the bread pan out of the machine, turn the bread out on to a wire rack and leave to cool completely.

White with Malted Grain

The granary-style or malted grain flour gives this white loaf some texture as well as a nutty flavour. The malt extract adds a subtle but lovely flavour.

1¼ tsp Easybake yeast
350g/12 oz strong white bread flour
150g/6 oz malted grain or granary-style flour
1¼ tsp fine sea salt
1 tbsp malt extract
350ml/12 fl oz water

1. Put the ingredients into the bread pan in the correct order for your machine.

2. Fit the pan into the bread machine and close the lid.

3. Select the BASIC WHITE setting, MEDIUM CRUST and the appropriate SIZE. Press Start.

4. When the program has finished, lift the bread pan out of the machine, turn the bread out on to a wire rack and leave to cool completely.

White with Rye

The addition of rye flour makes a slightly more dense loaf with a lovely soft crumb. To ensure success, don't be tempted to increase the amount of rye flour and always use a rapid program.

1 tsp Easybake yeast
385g/14 oz extra strong or Canadian white bread flour
115g/4 oz rye flour
1½ tsp fine sea salt
350ml/12 fl oz water

1. Put the ingredients into the bread pan in the correct order for your machine.

2. Fit the pan into the bread machine and close the lid.

3. Select the BASIC WHITE RAPID setting, DARK CRUST and the appropriate SIZE. Press Start.

4. When the program has finished, lift the bread pan out of the machine, turn the bread out on to a wire rack and leave to cool completely.

Spelt and White

In bread machines, spelt flour is best used in combination with strong white flour. If you want to make an all-spelt loaf, you will need to use the DOUGH program (using 300ml/½ pt water only), then shape the fairly sticky dough by hand and bake it in the oven (check the instructions on the spelt packet for the recommended oven temperature).

1 tsp Easybake yeast
250g/9 oz spelt flour
250g/9 oz strong white bread flour
1¼ tsp fine sea salt
350ml/12 fl oz water

1. Put the ingredients into the bread pan in the correct order for your machine.

2. Fit the pan into the bread machine and close the lid.

3. Select the BASIC WHITE setting, MEDIUM CRUST and the appropriate SIZE. Press Start.

4. When the program has finished, lift the bread pan out of the machine, turn the bread out on to a wire rack and leave to cool completely.

White with Polenta

This loaf has a moist texture and a lovely crisp, golden crust with just a slight hint of yellow. Slightly denser than ordinary white bread, it's particularly good served with soups and spiced dishes.

1 tsp Easybake yeast
375g/13 oz strong white bread flour
85g/3 oz polenta or cornmeal
1½ tsp fine sea salt
350ml/12 fl oz water
1 tbsp clear honey

1. Put the ingredients into the bread pan in the correct order for your machine.

2. Fit the pan into the bread machine and close the lid.

3. Select the BASIC WHITE setting, MEDIUM CRUST and the appropriate SIZE. Press Start.

4. When the program has finished, lift the bread pan out of the machine, turn the bread out on to a wire rack and leave to cool completely.

White with Buckwheat

A small amount of buckwheat gives this bread a distinctive flavour, a deep brown crust and a dark moist centre.

1 tsp Easybake yeast
400g/14 oz strong white bread flour
100g/4 oz buckwheat flour
1¼ tsp fine sea salt
350ml/12 fl oz water

1. Put the ingredients into the bread pan in the correct order for your machine.
2. Fit the pan into the bread machine and close the lid.
3. Select the BASIC WHITE setting, MEDIUM CRUST and the appropriate SIZE. Press Start.
4. When the program has finished, lift the bread pan out of the machine, turn the bread out on to a wire rack and leave to cool completely.

White with Bran

A friend of mine needs to increase her fibre intake for medical reasons but she can't resist white bread. This loaf helps to make a contribution in the right direction.

1 tsp Easybake yeast
500g/1 lb 2 oz strong white bread flour
4 tbsp wheat or oat bran
1 tsp fine sea salt
1 tbsp malt extract
1 tbsp olive oil
350ml/12 fl oz water

1. Put the ingredients into the bread pan in the correct order for your machine.
2. Fit the pan into the bread machine and close the lid.
3. Select the BASIC WHITE setting, MEDIUM CRUST and the appropriate SIZE. Press Start.
4. When the program has finished, lift the bread pan out of the machine, turn the bread out on to a wire rack and leave to cool completely.

Softgrain Loaf

This is basically a white loaf with kibbled grains to provide the additional texture. Clear honey could be used in place of malt extract or, for a more doughy texture, try molasses (with molasses, the mixture in the machine will be slightly sticky, but this is nothing to worry about).

1 tsp Easybake yeast
500g/1 lb 2 oz softgrain strong white bread flour
1¼ tsp fine sea salt
1 tbsp malt extract
350ml/12 fl oz water

1. Put the ingredients into the bread pan in the correct order for your machine.

2. Fit the pan into the bread machine and close the lid.

3. Select the BASIC WHITE setting, MEDIUM CRUST and the appropriate SIZE. Press Start.

4. When the program has finished, lift the bread pan out of the machine, turn the bread out on to a wire rack and leave to cool completely.

Oaty Loaf

I am quite addicted to this rustic-looking white loaf with added oats. It's substantial yet light and, though the volume isn't as great as a normal white loaf, the texture and flavour are superb. Use extra strong or Canadian white bread flour if you have it. Serve it with soup, cheese or indeed just about anything else. This recipe is not suitable for use with the delay timer.

1¼ tsp Easybake yeast
350g/12 oz strong white bread flour
150g/6 oz whole rolled porridge oats
1 tsp fine sea salt
350ml/12 fl oz water

1. Put the ingredients into the bread pan in the correct order for your machine.

2. Fit the pan into the bread machine and close the lid.

3. Select the BASIC WHITE setting, MEDIUM CRUST and the appropriate SIZE. Press Start.

4. When the program has finished, lift the bread pan out of the machine, turn the bread out on to a wire rack and leave to cool completely.

Granary-style Loaf

A lovely loaf with a nutty flavour, an interesting texture and a soft crumb. You will need to refer to the instruction book that comes with your bread machine – to check the most appropriate program for recipes using entirely granary-style flour.

1¼ tsp Easybake yeast
500g/1 lb 2 oz granary-style or malted grain flour
1 tsp fine sea salt
2 tsp malt extract
1 tbsp sunflower or olive oil
350ml/12 fl oz water

1. Put the ingredients into the bread pan in the correct order for your machine.

2. Fit the pan into the bread machine and close the lid.

3. Select the BASIC WHITE or BASIC WHOLEWHEAT setting (check with the instruction book for your bread machine), MEDIUM CRUST and the appropriate SIZE. Press Start.

4. When the program has finished, lift the bread pan out of the machine, turn the bread out on to a wire rack and leave to cool completely.

Brown Bread

Here is a loaf that is fuller in flavour and slightly denser than a white loaf, yet is somewhat lighter than wholemeal bread.

1¼ tsp Easybake yeast
500g/1 lb 2 oz strong brown bread flour
1 tsp fine sea salt
2 tsp muscovado or unrefined brown sugar
1 tbsp sunflower or olive oil
350ml/12 fl oz water

1. Put the ingredients into the bread pan in the correct order for your machine.

2. Fit the pan into the bread machine and close the lid.

3. Scloct the BASIC WHITE setting, MEDIUM CRUST and the appropriate SIZE. Press Start.

4. When the program has finished, lift the bread pan out of the machine, turn the bread out on to a wire rack and leave to cool completely.

Wholemeal Loaf

There is a delicious, full flavour to this bread. It has a denser texture than a loaf made with white or granary-style flour and there is a lovely contrast between the crisp crust and the moist crumb. The vitamin C powder is optional but it does help to produce a larger, and therefore lighter, loaf (see page 23). If preferred, you could use 1-2 teaspoons of fresh lemon juice in its place (and reduce the water by the same amount).

1½ tsp Easybake yeast
500g/1 lb 2 oz wholemeal strong bread flour
1¼ tsp fine sea salt
¼ tsp vitamin C powder (optional)
1 tbsp malt extract
375ml/13 fl oz water

1. Put the ingredients into the bread pan in the correct order for your machine.

2. Fit the pan into the bread machine and close the lid.

3. Select the BASIC WHOLEWHEAT setting, MEDIUM CRUST and the appropriate SIZE. Press Start.

4. When the program has finished, lift the bread pan out of the machine, turn the bread out on to a wire rack and leave to cool completely.

Multi-grain Loaf

This is a good way to use up odds and ends of flour. The loaf often has a split, craggy top that looks quite rustic. It's very crusty with an excellent flavour and texture. Served with a bowl of soup or a chunk of cheese, it makes a filling meal.

1 tsp Easybake yeast
200g/7 oz strong white bread flour
100g/4 oz granary-style or malted grain flour
100g/3½ oz strong wholemeal flour
100g/3½ oz rye flour
1¼ tsp fine sea salt
1 tbsp clear honey
1 tbsp olive oil
335ml/11½ fl oz water

1. Put the ingredients into the bread pan in the correct order for your machine.

2. Fit the pan into the bread machine and close the lid.

3. Select the BASIC WHITE setting, MEDIUM CRUST and the appropriate SIZE. Press Start.

4. When the program has finished, lift the bread pan out of the machine, turn the bread out on to a wire rack and leave to cool completely.

Milk Loaf

This light loaf has a crisp deep-golden crust and a soft smooth crumb. It keeps well and makes good toast. You can, of course, use 350ml/12 fl oz fresh milk in place of the water and milk powder which will produce a slightly closer texture. Make sure the milk is at room temperature (or lukewarm if your bread machines requires it) and do not use the delay timer.

1 tsp Easybake yeast
500g/1 lb 2 oz strong white bread flour
1 tsp fine sea salt
1 tsp golden caster sugar
4 tbsp dried skimmed milk powder
350ml/12 fl oz water
25g/1 oz butter, cut into small pieces

1. Put the ingredients into the bread pan in the correct order for your machine.

2. Fit the pan into the bread machine and close the lid.

3. Select the BASIC WHITE setting, MEDIUM CRUST and the appropriate SIZE. Press Start.

4. When the program has finished, lift the bread pan out of the machine, turn the bread out on to a wire rack and leave to cool completely.

Half-and-Half with Buttermilk

This rustic-looking loaf has a craggy top and a slightly acidic flavour, rather like soda bread. If you cannot find buttermilk, use low-fat natural yogurt. This recipe is not suitable for use with the delay timer.

1¼ tsp Easybake yeast
250g/9 oz strong white bread flour
250g/9 oz strong wholemeal bread flour
1 tsp fine sea salt
1 tbsp clear honey
284ml carton buttermilk
135ml/4½ fl oz water

1. Put the ingredients into the bread pan in the correct order for your machine.

2. Fit the pan into the bread machine and close the lid.

3. Select the BASIC WHITE setting, MEDIUM CRUST and the appropriate SIZE. Press Start.

4. When the program has finished, lift the bread pan out of the machine, turn the bread out on to a wire rack and leave to cool completely.

LOAVES WITH ATTITUDE

(OR BREADS PACKED WITH FLAVOUR)

Adding extra ingredients to bread can transform it into something really special, altering its colour, texture and flavour. In this section you will find my favourite recipes – from loaves that are lightly perfumed to more robust ones with assertive flavours. There are ideas for using herbs, spices, seeds, nuts, fruit, vegetables, honey, mustard, beer and even chocolate.

I'd like to think that you will use my recipes as inspiration for your own flavour combinations. This is where you can be really creative, inventing your own breads with wonderful flavours to impress family and friends.

Sun-dried Tomato and Rosemary Loaf

I am often disappointed with tomato-flavoured breads – the flavour can be overpowering, particularly when served as part of a meal. I am really pleased with this one because the flavour is delicate, the texture is soft and smooth, and the crust is crisp yet light. It makes delicious sandwiches and freezes well. For a more gutsy flavour, try the Robust Tomato Loaf opposite.

1 tsp Easybake yeast
350g/12 oz strong white bread flour
150g/6 oz granary-type or malted grain flour
1 tsp fine sea salt
320ml/11 fl oz water
55g/2 oz sun-dried tomatoes in oil, drained and finely
  chopped
2 tbsp tomato oil (from the jar of sun-dried tomatoes)
1 tbsp finely chopped fresh rosemary

1. Put all the ingredients into the bread pan in the correct order for your machine.

2. Fit the pan into the bread machine and close the lid.

3. Select the BASIC WHITE setting, MEDIUM CRUST and the appropriate SIZE. Press Start.

4. When the program has finished, lift the bread pan out of the machine, turn the bread out on to a wire rack and leave to cool completely.

Robust Tomato Loaf

The deep rich colour of this bread is an indication of its intense tomato flavour. I like to add the tomatoes part way through the program (at the beeping sound) so that some of the pieces remain whole. If you want to make the bread overnight, adding the tomatoes at the start, it simply means that the finished colour and flavour will be more evenly distributed through the loaf. Rest assured, it will still taste wonderful. Serve it with mozzarella and black olives, well-flavoured cheeses or roasted vegetables. If you prefer a more delicate flavour and smooth texture, try the Sun-dried Tomato and Rosemary Loaf opposite which uses sun-dried tomatoes in oil.

1 tsp Easybake yeast
350g/12 oz strong white bread flour
150g/6 oz granary-type or malted grain flour
1 tsp fine sea salt
320ml/11 fl oz water
2 tbsp olive oil
100g packet soft-dried (mi-cuit) tomatoes, quartered

1. Put all the ingredients, except for the tomatoes, into the bread pan in the correct order for your machine.

2. Fit the pan into the bread machine and close the lid.

3. Select the BASIC WHITE RAISIN setting, MEDIUM CRUST and the appropriate SIZE. Press Start. When the machine indicates (with a beeping sound), add the tomatoes and close the lid again.

4. When the program has finished, lift the bread pan out of the machine, turn the bread out on to a wire rack and leave to cool completely.

Toasted Sunflower Seed and Honey Loaf

This bread has a crisp crust and a lovely texture that is provided by the sunflower seeds. I enjoy the nutty flavour and the vague suggestion of sweetness from the honey.

1 tsp Easybake yeast
350g/12 oz strong white bread flour
150g/6 oz granary-type or malted grain flour
1 tsp fine sea salt
350ml/12 fl oz water
2 tbsp clear honey
5 tbsp sesame seeds, toasted until lightly browned

1. Put all the ingredients, except for the seeds, into the bread pan in the correct order for your machine.

2. Fit the pan into the bread machine and close the lid.

3. Select the BASIC WHITE RAISIN setting, MEDIUM CRUST and the appropriate SIZE. Press Start. When the machine indicates (with a beeping sound), add the seeds and close the lid again.

4. When the program has finished, lift the bread pan out of the machine, turn the bread out on to a wire rack and leave to cool completely.

Mixed Seed Loaf

If, like me, you like the texture and flavour that seeds give to bread, you will enjoy this loaf. The sesame oil adds extra flavour though you could of course use olive oil instead.

1¼ tsp Easybake yeast
250g/9 oz strong white bread flour
250g/9 oz strong wholemeal flour
1 tsp fine sea salt
350ml/12 fl oz water
1 tbsp sesame oil
1 tbsp clear honey (use one with a good, pronounced flavour)
85g/3 oz mixed seeds (sunflower, pumpkin, sesame and poppy)

1. Put all the ingredients, except for the seeds, into the bread pan in the correct order for your machine.

2. Fit the pan into the bread machine and close the lid.

3. Select the BASIC WHOLEWHEAT RAISIN setting, MEDIUM CRUST and the appropriate SIZE. Press Start. When the machine indicates (with a beeping sound), add the seeds and close the lid again.

4. When the program has finished, lift the bread pan out of the machine, turn the bread out on to a wire rack and leave to cool completely.

Walnut Bread

This bread, with its distinctive flavour of walnuts, is delicious served just as it is, with butter for spreading or olive oil for dipping. The addition of walnut oil really boosts the flavour, though, if you prefer, you could replace it with olive oil.

1¼ tsp Easybake yeast
250g/9 oz strong white bread flour
250g/9 oz strong wholemeal flour
1 tsp fine sea salt
350ml/12 fl oz water
1 tbsp walnut oil
1 tbsp honey (use one with a good, pronounced flavour)
115g/4 oz broken walnuts

1. Put all the ingredients, except for the walnuts, into the bread pan in the correct order for your machine.

2. Fit the pan into the bread machine and close the lid.

3. Select the BASIC WHOLEWHEAT RAISIN setting, MEDIUM CRUST and the appropriate SIZE. Press Start. When the machine indicates (with a beeping sound), add the walnuts and close the lid again.

4. When the program has finished, lift the bread pan out of the machine, turn the bread out on to a wire rack and leave to cool completely.

Chilli Bread

This is bread with a surprise kick! Make it as hot as you wish by adjusting the quantity of chillies and serve it with cheese, soup or (my favourite) sausages.

1¼ tsp Easybake yeast
250g/9 oz strong wholemeal bread flour
250g/9 oz strong white bread flour
1 tsp fine sea salt
1 tbsp muscovado sugar
2 tsp crushed chillies, or to taste
350ml/12 fl oz water

1. Put the ingredients into the bread pan in the correct order for your machine.

2. Fit the pan into the bread machine and close the lid.

3. Select the BASIC WHOLEWHEAT setting, MEDIUM CRUST and the appropriate SIZE. Press Start.

4. When the program has finished, lift the bread pan out of the machine, turn the bread out on to a wire rack and leave to cool completely.

Moroccan Spice Loaf

This bread has a slightly exotic perfume and a sweet spicy crumb. It is delicious served with lamb and vegetable dishes. Ras el hanout is a complex blend of spices that can include anise, cardamom, cinnamon, cloves, galangal ginger, mace, nigella, nutmeg, peppercorns, turmeric and dried flowers (such as damask rose). Look out for it in the 'specials' area of large supermarkets, in delicatessens or in specialist food shops.

1 tsp Easybake yeast
450g/1 lb strong white bread flour
50g/2 oz cornmeal or polenta
1¼ tsp fine sea salt
2 tsp ras el hanout (Moroccan spice blend)
2 tsp clear honey
350ml/12 fl oz water

1. Put the ingredients into the bread pan in the correct order for your machine.

2. Fit the pan into the bread machine and close the lid.

3. Select the BASIC WHITE setting, MEDIUM CRUST and the appropriate SIZE. Press Start.

4. When the program has finished, lift the bread pan out of the machine, turn the bread out on to a wire rack and leave to cool completely.

Chocolate Loaf

It has a crisp crust with a light crumb and its colour is, well, chocolaty! It is particularly good served with game dishes such as venison and pheasant casseroles, though my family likes it for breakfast with strong coffee or made into a banana sandwich at any other time of the day. Lovers of bitter chocolate might like to try adding an extra 25g/1 oz cocoa (and reducing the flour by 25g/1 oz) – the colour will be amazing and the flavour strong.

1 tsp Easybake yeast
450g/1 lb strong white bread flour
50g/2 oz cocoa powder
1 tsp fine sea salt
2 tbsp muscovado sugar
25g/1 oz butter, cut into small pieces
350ml/12 fl oz water

1. Put the ingredients into the bread pan in the correct order for your machine.

2. Fit the pan into the bread machine and close the lid.

3. Select the BASIC WHITE setting, MEDIUM CRUST and the appropriate SIZE. Press Start.

4. When the program has finished, lift the bread pan out of the machine, turn the bread out on to a wire rack and leave to cool completely.

Banana Bread

The banana imparts a delicate flavour and colour and a slightly stretchy crumb. I like to eat this bread still warm and just as it is, but it's particularly good with crisp-cooked bacon too. Or try thick slices toasted and topped with soft berry fruit, a drizzle of runny honey and served with ice cream. This recipe is not suitable for delayed programs.

1¼ tsp Easybake yeast
350g/12 oz strong white bread flour
150g/6 oz strong wholemeal flour
1 tsp fine sea salt
2 medium bananas (total 250-275g/9-9½ oz before peeling), mashed
2 tbsp clear honey
1 medium egg, beaten
15g/½ oz butter, cut into small pieces
250ml/9 fl oz water
½ tsp vanilla extract (optional)

1. Put the ingredients into the bread pan in the correct order for your machine.

2. Fit the pan into the bread machine and close the lid.

3. Select the BASIC WHITE setting, LIGHT CRUST and the appropriate SIZE. Press Start. As it mixes, the dough will be moist and sticky – you may need to scrape down the sides in order to make sure that all the mixture is incorporated.

4. When the program has finished, lift the bread pan out of the machine. Leave to cool for 10-15 minutes before turning the bread out on to a wire rack and leaving to cool completely.

Cheese and Wholegrain Mustard Loaf

A filling loaf that makes a comforting meal served with grilled sausages and a salad of fresh tomatoes and onion slices. Do not use the delay timer for this recipe.

1 tsp Easybake yeast
400g/14 oz strong white bread flour
100g/4 oz strong wholemeal flour
1 tsp fine sea salt
2 tsp clear honey
1 tbsp wholegrain mustard
350ml/12 fl oz water
115g/4 oz mature Cheddar cheese, grated

1. Put all the ingredients, except for the cheese, into the bread pan in the correct order for your machine.

2. Fit the pan into the bread machine and close the lid.

3. Select the BASIC WHITE RAISIN setting, MEDIUM CRUST and the appropriate SIZE. Press Start. When the machine indicates (with a beeping sound), add the cheese and close the lid again.

4. When the program has finished, lift the bread pan out of the machine, turn the bread out on to a wire rack and leave to cool completely.

Sage and Onion Loaf

Sounds like stuffing, right? You will be pleasantly surprised by the subtle flavour combination in this bread. It makes a perfect partner for chicken, pork or sausages.

25g/1 oz butter
1 large onion, finely chopped
1 tsp Easybake yeast
250g/9 oz strong white bread flour
250g/9 oz strong wholemeal flour
1 tsp fine sea salt
¼ tsp freshly ground black pepper
350ml/12 fl oz water
2 tbsp chopped fresh sage or 1 tbsp dried

1. Melt the butter in a pan, add the onion and cook gently for about 10 minutes, stirring occasionally, until very soft but not browned. Alternatively, put the butter and onion into a casserole, cover and microwave on HIGH for 5 minutes, stirring once, until very soft. Leave to cool.

2. Put the remaining ingredients into the bread pan in the correct order for your machine. Add the buttery onion mixture.

3. Fit the pan into the bread machine and close the lid.

4. Select the BASIC WHITE setting, MEDIUM CRUST and the appropriate SIZE. Press Start.

5. When the program has finished, lift the bread pan out of the machine, turn the bread out on to a wire rack and leave to cool completely.

Minted Bread

The slight sweetness in this loaf comes from the apple juice. Why not serve it with cheese, chicken, pork or sausages, or use it to make a refreshing cucumber or salad sandwich?

1 tsp Easybake yeast
400g/14 oz strong white bread flour
100g/4 oz strong wholemeal bread flour
½ tsp fine sea salt
2 tbsp finely chopped fresh mint or 2 tsp dried mint
350ml/12 fl oz apple juice

1. Put the ingredients into the bread pan in the correct order for your machine.

2. Fit the pan into the bread machine and close the lid.

3. Select the BASIC WHITE setting, MEDIUM CRUST and the appropriate SIZE. Press Start.

4. When the program has finished, lift the bread pan out of the machine, turn the bread out on to a wire rack and leave to cool completely.

Toasted Pine Nut and Pesto Bread

This loaf has a lovely light crust and a subtle flavour. Serve it with soups and all manner of Italian delicatessen.

1 tsp Easybake yeast
500g/1 lb 2 oz strong white bread flour
1 tsp fine sea salt
3 tbsp green pesto (from a jar)
330ml/11 fl oz water
40g/1½ oz pine nuts, toasted

1. Put the ingredients, except for the pine nuts, into the bread pan in the correct order for your machine.

2. Fit the pan into the bread machine and close the lid.

3. Select the BASIC WHITE RAISIN setting, MEDIUM CRUST and the appropriate SIZE. Press Start. When the machine indicates (with a beeping sound), add the pine nuts and close the lid again.

4. When the program has finished, lift the bread pan out of the machine, turn the bread out on to a wire rack and leave to cool completely.

Spiced Cranberry Bread

I often make this at Christmas and use it for sandwiches filled with cold turkey or chicken, or Brie and salad leaves. No buttermilk? Use low-fat natural yogurt instead. This recipe is not suitable for use with the timer.

1½ tsp Easybake yeast
400g/14 oz strong white bread flour
100g/4 oz strong wholemeal bread flour
¾ tsp fine sea salt
1 tsp ground mixed spice
½ tsp bicarbonate of soda
1 tbsp clear honey
25g/1 oz butter, cut into small pieces
284ml carton buttermilk
120ml/4 fl oz water
85g/3 oz dried cranberries

1. Put all the ingredients, except the cranberries, into the bread pan in the correct order for your machine.

2. Fit the pan into the bread machine and close the lid.

3. Select the BASIC WHITE RAISIN setting, MEDIUM CRUST and the appropriate SIZE. Press Start. When the machine indicates (with a beeping sound), add the cranberries and close the lid again.

4. When the program has finished, lift the bread pan out of the machine, turn the bread out on to a wire rack and leave to cool completely.

Porter Bread

This was a real winner with all my tasters. Bread made with beer has a very crisp and shiny crust and tastes delicious. The best flavour (in my opinion anyway) comes from a dark brown ale that has some sweetness, such as Porter or stout. On breaking the bread, you can really smell the malty tones of the beer. If you prefer a lighter flavour and texture, try a pale ale instead. This loaf is best eaten on the day it is made – if you need to keep it longer, add 1-2 tbsp oil in step 1. My family particularly likes it as part of a "ploughman's" plate of cheese and pickles.

1 tsp Easybake yeast
400g/14 oz strong white bread flour
100g/4 oz strong wholemeal bread flour
1 tsp fine sea salt
1 tbsp clear honey
350ml/12 fl oz Porter, stout or pale ale (poured and left
  to stand for 5 minutes)

1. Put the ingredients into the bread pan in the correct order for your machine.

2. Fit the pan into the bread machine and close the lid.

3. Select the BASIC WHITE setting, MEDIUM CRUST and the appropriate SIZE. Press Start.

4. When the program has finished, lift the bread pan out of the machine, turn the bread out on to a wire rack and leave to cool completely.

Cheddar and Rosemary Loaf

A savoury bread that is good served warm or at room temperature with vegetable soups, meat, poultry or sausages. This recipe is best not cooked using the delay timer.

1 tsp Easybake yeast
400g/14 oz strong white bread flour
100g/4 oz strong wholemeal flour
1 tsp fine sea salt
1 tsp golden caster sugar
1 tbsp finely chopped fresh rosemary leaves
350ml/12 fl oz water
115g/4 oz mature Cheddar cheese, grated

1. Put all the ingredients, except for the cheese, into the bread pan in the correct order for your machine.

2. Fit the pan into the bread machine and close the lid.

3. Select the BASIC WHITE RAISIN setting, MEDIUM CRUST and the appropriate SIZE. Press Start. When the machine indicates (with a beeping sound), add the cheese and close the lid again.

4. When the program has finished, lift the bread pan out of the machine, turn the bread out on to a wire rack and leave to cool completely.

Trio of Herbs

Vary the herbs to suit your own preference, the season and your herb garden. Particular favourites of mine are fennel (good with fish) and tarragon (makes an aromatic chicken sandwich).

1 tsp Easybake yeast
500g/1 lb 2 oz strong white bread flour
1 tsp fine sea salt
1 tbsp malt extract
2 tbsp chopped fresh parsley
1 tbsp fresh thyme leaves
2 tbsp snipped chives
1 tbsp olive oil
350ml/12 fl oz water

1. Put the ingredients into the bread pan in the correct order for your machine.

2. Fit the pan into the bread machine and close the lid.

3. Select the BASIC WHITE setting, MEDIUM CRUST and the appropriate SIZE. Press Start.

4. When the program has finished, lift the bread pan out of the machine, turn the bread out on to a wire rack and leave to cool completely.

Hazelnut and Cinnamon Bread

This is a lovely tea-time bread, served sliced and spread with butter. It makes a lovely dessert too – toast thick slices, top them with lightly cooked fresh fruit such as raspberries or apricots and add a dollop of crème fraîche and a drizzle of honey.

1¼ tsp Easybake yeast
250g/9 oz extra strong or Canadian white bread flour
250g/9 oz strong wholemeal flour
1 tsp fine sea salt
¾ tsp ground cinnamon
350ml/12 fl oz water
1 tbsp walnut oil
1 tbsp clear honey
115g/4 oz hazelnuts, toasted and finely chopped

1. Put all the ingredients, except for the hazelnuts, into the bread pan in the correct order for your machine.

2. Fit the pan into the bread machine and close the lid.

3. Select the BASIC WHOLEWHEAT RAISIN setting, MEDIUM CRUST and the appropriate SIZE. Press Start. When the machine indicates (with a beeping sound), add the hazelnuts and close the lid again.

4. When the program has finished, lift the bread pan out of the machine, turn the bread out on to a wire rack and leave to cool completely.

Coriander and Chilli Bread

The sweetness of the coconut really complements the mild heat of the chillies and the fresh perfume of the coriander. Leave out the chillies and coriander and you have a light loaf that is quite delicious served with Thai-style dishes. Or try toasting thick slices, sprinkling with sugar and serving with sliced ripe bananas. Don't be tempted to use the delay timer for this recipe.

1 tsp Easybake yeast
500g/1 lb 2 oz strong white bread flour
¾ tsp salt
150ml/¼ pt coconut milk
150ml/¼ pt water
2 mild green chillies, seeds removed, and finely chopped
Handful of chopped fresh coriander

1. Put all the ingredients, except for the chillies and coriander, into the bread pan in the correct order for your machine.

2. Fit the pan into the bread machine and close the lid.

3. Select the BASIC WHITE RAISIN setting, MEDIUM CRUST and the appropriate SIZE. Press Start. When the machine indicates (with a beeping sound), add the chillies and coriander and close the lid again.

4. When the program has finished, lift the bread pan out of the machine, turn the bread out on to a wire rack and leave to cool completely.

THE KITCHEN BAKER

(OR HAND-SHAPED, OVEN-BAKED BREADS)

For those of us who enjoy working with dough, this is the section. Here you will find rolls and flatbreads, hand-shaped loaves, sweet doughs and other speciality bread.

How many of us I wonder would normally contemplate making bread rolls, focaccia, pitta or flatbreads in time for a meal just a few hours away? There just wouldn't be enough time to do all that mixing, kneading, shaping, rising and baking as well as go shopping, pick the children up from school, have a shower and prepare the rest of the meal. With a bread machine, you can do it all.

While the bread machine does the time-consuming part – mixing, kneading and proving the dough – you get on with other things. Once the dough is ready, just shape it by hand, leave it to rise and then bake it in a hot oven. Some dough, like flatbread, does not even need to rise first.

White Rolls

Just listen to the crusts crackling when these rolls come out of the oven. Resist them if you can!

Makes 12

1 tsp Easybake yeast
500g/1 lb 2 oz strong white bread flour
1 tsp fine sea salt
300ml/½ pt water

1. Put the ingredients into the bread pan in the correct order for your machine.

2. Fit the pan into the bread machine and close the lid.

3. Select the WHITE DOUGH setting and the SIZE if appropriate. Press Start.

4. When the program has finished, turn the dough on to a lightly floured surface and knead lightly, knocking out the air, until smooth and elastic.

5. Divide the dough into 12 equal pieces and, with floured hands, shape into rolls. Arrange, smooth side up, on a greased baking sheet.

6. Cover with oiled film and leave to rise until doubled in size.

7. Meanwhile, preheat the oven to 220°C (Fan 200°C), 425°F, Gas 7.

8. Remove the film, put into the hot oven and cook for about 15 minutes until golden brown and cooked through.

9. Transfer to a wire rack and leave to cool.

White Rolls with Granary

My family describes these essentially white rolls as 'light with bits in'. They have a delicious crust and an airy centre. Adding milk powder will produce a texture that is slightly more close.

Makes 12

1 tsp Easybake yeast
350g/12 oz strong white bread flour
150g/6 oz granary-style or malted flour, plus extra for dusting
1 tsp fine sea salt
2 tsp malt extract
1 tbsp milk powder (optional)
15g/½ oz butter, cut into small pieces
300ml/½ pt water

1. Put the ingredients into the bread pan in the correct order for your machine.

2. Fit the pan into the bread machine and close the lid.

3. Select the WHITE DOUGH setting and the SIZE if appropriate. Press Start.

4. When the program has finished, turn the dough on to a lightly floured surface and knead lightly, knocking out the air, until smooth and elastic.

5. Cut the dough into 12 pieces and shape into rolls. Arrange, smooth side up and spaced about 2.5cm/1 in apart, on a greased baking tray.

6. Cover with oiled film and leave to rise until doubled in size.

7. Meanwhile, preheat the oven to 220°C (Fan 200°C), 425°F, Gas 7.

8. Remove the film and dust the tops with a little extra flour.

9. Put into the hot oven and cook for about 15 minutes until golden brown and cooked through. Transfer to a wire rack and leave to cool.

Wholemeal Rolls

I particularly enjoy eating these while they are still slightly warm, though the lovely nutty flavour is equally delicious when they are cold. The dough needs to be quite moist (in order not to overwork the bread machine) so, the first time you make these rolls, monitor the mixing process, adding a little extra liquid if necessary. I think the small amount of oil improves this recipe but leave it out if you prefer.

Makes 10

1 tsp Easybake yeast
500g/1 lb 2 oz strong wholemeal flour, plus extra for
   dusting
1¼ tsp fine sea salt
2 tsp malt extract
1 tbsp olive oil
350ml/12 fl oz water (or half water and half milk)

1. Put the ingredients into the bread pan in the correct order for your machine.

2. Fit the pan into the bread machine and close the lid.

3. Select the WHOLEWHEAT DOUGH setting and the SIZE if appropriate. Press Start.

4. When the program has finished, turn the dough on to a floured surface and knead lightly, knocking out the air, until smooth.

5. Cut the dough into 10 pieces and, keeping the surface floured, shape into rolls, flattening them slightly to look like baps. Arrange, smooth side up and spaced about 2.5cm/1 in apart, on a greased baking sheet.

6. Cover with oiled film and leave to rise until doubled in size.

7. Meanwhile, preheat the oven to 200°C (Fan 180°C), 400°F, Gas 6.

8. Remove the film and dust the rolls with a little extra flour.

9. Put into the hot oven and cook for 15-20 minutes until golden brown and cooked through.

10. Transfer to a wire rack and leave to cool.

Bridge Rolls

These small slim rolls are enriched with egg and have a soft crust. Children love them.

Makes about 24

1 small egg
Milk
1 tsp Easybake yeast
500g/1 lb 2 oz strong white bread flour
1 tsp fine sea salt
1 tbsp golden caster sugar
40g/1½ oz butter, cut into small pieces
Beaten egg, to glaze

1. Lightly beat the egg and make up to 300ml/½ pt with milk.

2. Put the ingredients, including the egg mixture, into the bread pan in the correct order for your machine.

3. Fit the pan into the bread machine and close the lid.

4. Select the WHITE DOUGH setting and the SIZE if appropriate. Press Start.

5. When the program has finished, turn the dough on to a lightly floured surface and knead lightly, knocking out the air, until smooth and elastic.

6. Cut the dough into 24 pieces and shape into fingers. Arrange, smooth side up and quite close together, on a greased baking tray.

7. Cover with oiled film and leave to rise until doubled in size (this should take only 15-20 minutes).

8. Meanwhile, preheat the oven to 220°C (Fan 200°C), 425°F, Gas 7.

9. Remove the film and brush the tops gently with the beaten egg glaze.

10. Put into the hot oven and cook for about 15 minutes until golden brown and cooked through. Transfer to a wire rack and leave to cool.

Huffkins

I love the name of these funny flat rolls with a dimple in the middle, sometimes called Kentish Huffkins. They are oval in shape, have a soft crust and are usually made with all white flour. As you can see, I like to use a small amount of wholemeal flour too.

Makes 12

1 tsp Easybake yeast
300g/10½ oz strong white bread flour
150g/5½ oz strong wholemeal flour
1 tsp fine sea salt
2 tsp golden caster sugar
50g/1¾ oz butter, cut into small pieces
250ml/9 fl oz milk and water mixed

1. Put the ingredients into the bread pan in the correct order for your machine.

2. Fit the pan into the bread machine and close the lid.

3. Select the WHITE DOUGH setting and the SIZE if appropriate. Press Start.

4. When the program has finished, turn the dough on to a lightly floured surface and knead lightly, knocking out the air, until smooth and elastic.

5. Cut the dough into 12 equal pieces and roll into ovals about 1cm/½ in thick. Arrange, smooth side up and with plenty of room between, on lightly greased baking trays.

6. Cover with a tea towel and leave to rise until doubled in size.

7. Meanwhile, preheat the oven to 220°C (Fan 200°C), 425°F, Gas 7.

8. Remove the towel and, just before baking, make a deep thumb mark in the centre of each piece of dough.

9. Put into the hot oven and cook for about 15 minutes until golden brown and cooked through.

10. Wrap in a warm tea towel (to keep the crusts soft) and leave to cool.

Granary Baps

Serve these soft flat rolls with your favourite filling. They are ideal for picnics and packed lunches.

Makes 8-10

1 tsp Easybake yeast
500g/1 lb 2 oz granary-style or malted flour
1 tsp fine sea salt
1 tbsp malt extract
150ml/¼ pt water
150ml/¼ pt milk
Rolled oats for topping

1. Put all the ingredients, except the oats, into the bread pan in the correct order for your machine.

2. Fit the pan into the bread machine and close the lid.

3. Select the WHITE DOUGH setting and the SIZE if appropriate. Press Start.

4. When the program has finished, turn the dough on to a lightly floured surface and knead lightly, knocking out the air, until smooth and elastic.

5. Cut the dough into 8-10 pieces and shape into balls. Flatten the balls to about 10cm/4 in diameter. Arrange, smooth side up and spaced about 2.5cm/1 in apart, on a greased baking tray.

6. Cover with oiled film and leave to rise until doubled in size.

7. Meanwhile, preheat the oven to 220°C (Fan 200°C), 425°F, Gas 7.

8. Remove the film, lightly brush the tops with water and sprinkle with rolled oats.

9. Put into the hot oven and cook for about 20 minutes until golden brown and cooked through.

10. Transfer to a wire rack and leave to cool.

Pizza Dough

Makes one large or two smaller pizza bases. They can be frozen at the end of step 5 – thaw at room temperature, add the toppings and continue.

1 tsp Easybake yeast
450g/1 lb strong white bread flour
1 tsp salt
250ml/9 fl oz water
2 tbsp olive oil

1. Put the ingredients into the bread pan in the correct order for your machine. Fit the pan into the bread machine and close the lid.

2. Select the PIZZA, QUICK DOUGH or WHITE DOUGH setting and the SIZE if appropriate. Press Start.

3. When the program has finished, turn the dough on to a lightly floured surface and knead, knocking out the air, until smooth and elastic.

4. Using a rolling pin or your hands, roll or push the dough out into one large or two smaller circles (this will need patience and perseverance because the dough will keep shrinking back again). I like a thin crust but you can decide just how thin to make it.

5. Put the pizza base(s) on to one or two lightly oiled baking trays, cover with oiled clear film or a damp (warm) tea towel and leave to rise for about 15 minutes while you prepare the toppings.

6. Meanwhile, preheat the oven to 200°C (Fan 180°C), 400°F, Gas 6.

7. Spread your chosen toppings (see opposite) over the dough, leaving the edges free.

8. Put into the hot oven and cook for about 15 minutes until the edges are puffed up and crisp, the toppings are golden brown and the pizza base is cooked through.

Toppings

Spread the pizza bases with sieved tomatoes (passata) and top with

- Torn basil leaves, sliced mozzarella and a drizzle of olive oil.

- Black olives, drained anchovy fillets, thinly sliced mozzarella and a drizzle of olive oil.

- Drained canned artichoke hearts (quartered), drained capers and flakes of Parmesan cheese.

- Thinly sliced tomatoes, fresh thyme leaves and Parma ham.

- Chorizo (or spicy sausage) slices, rosemary and freshly grated Parmesan or mature Cheddar cheese.

Pizza Stuffed with Cheese, Tomato and Herbs

A delicious hot 'sandwich' of which, I warn you, one piece is never enough. Serve it hot, cut into wedges. And when you want a change, vary the fillings: try ham, cheese and chopped fresh sage; thinly sliced red onion with your favourite cheese and some fresh rosemary leaves; or toasted pine nuts, caramelised onions, feta cheese and fresh thyme.

1 tsp Easybake yeast
450g/1 lb strong white bread flour
1 tsp salt
250ml/9 fl oz water
2 tbsp olive oil
About 12 cherry tomatoes, halved
200g/7 oz mozzarella, thinly sliced
1 tbsp dried oregano, plus a little extra
Freshly milled black pepper
Extra olive oil
Sea salt flakes

1. Put yeast, flour, salt, water and 2 tbsp oil into the bread pan in the correct order for your machine. Fit the pan into the bread machine and close the lid.

2. Select the PIZZA, QUICK DOUGH or WHITE DOUGH setting and the SIZE if appropriate. Press Start.

3. When the program has finished, turn the dough on to a lightly floured surface and knead, knocking out the air, until smooth and elastic.

4. Divide the dough into two equal pieces. Using a rolling pin or your hands, roll or push the first piece of dough into a large thin circle (be patient and persevere as the dough keeps shrinking back again).

5. Put the pizza base on to a lightly oiled baking tray.

6. Arrange the tomatoes, mozzarella and oregano over the top, spreading them right up to the edges. Season with black pepper.

7. Roll or push the remaining dough into a circle to match the first. Lay it on top of the filling and pinch the edges together to seal them.

8. Cover with oiled clear film or a damp (warm) tea towel and leave to rise for about 20 minutes.

9. Meanwhile, preheat the oven to 200°C (Fan 180°C), 400°F, Gas 6.

10. Drizzle some oil over the top and top with a light sprinkling of oregano and salt flakes.

11. Put into the hot oven and cook for about 20 minutes or until crisp and golden brown.

Two-cheese and Tomato Purses

Though these little bread 'pasties' look filling, they are really quite light. I serve them with a large green salad dressed with oil and vinegar. Vary the fillings to suit the contents of your fridge – try adding some finely chopped ham or salami, or some caramelised onions or roasted peppers, or replace the ricotta cheese with mozzarella. The choice is entirely yours.

Makes 8

1 tsp Easybake yeast
500g/1 lb 2 oz strong white bread flour
1½ tsp fine sea salt
½ tsp golden caster sugar
250ml/9 fl oz water
4 tbsp olive oil
250g carton ricotta cheese
6 tbsp freshly grated Parmesan cheese
6 sun-dried tomatoes in oil, drained and finely chopped
2 tsp dried oregano
Salt and freshly milled black pepper

1. Put the first six ingredients into the bread pan in the correct order for your machine. Fit the pan into the bread machine and close the lid.

2. Select the PIZZA, QUICK DOUGH or WHITE DOUGH setting and the SIZE if appropriate. Press Start.

3. Meanwhile, combine the two cheeses, tomatoes and oregano, seasoning to taste with salt and pepper.

4. When the program has finished, turn the dough on to a lightly floured surface and knead, knocking out the air, until smooth and elastic.

5. Divide the dough into eight equal pieces. Using a rolling pin or your hands, roll or push the first piece of dough into a circle measuring about 15cm/6 in (if you find the dough keeps shrinking back again, leave it to relax for 5 minutes before trying again).

6. Put a spoonful of the cheese filling on to each circle. Fold the dough over the filling, and pinch the edges

together (brush the edge with a little water if necessary to encourage it to stick) to make 'pasty' shapes.

7. Place on a lightly oiled baking sheet, cover with a damp (warm) tea towel and leave to rise for about 20 minutes.

8. Meanwhile, preheat the oven to 220°C (Fan 200°C), 425°F, Gas 7.

9. Put into the hot oven and cook for about 12 minutes until golden brown and cooked through.

10. Leave to stand for 5-10 minutes and serve immediately.

Focaccia with Oregano

An Italian flatbread that's really easy to make and is always a favourite in our family. Serve it warm, split and filled with roast vegetables, ham, salami, cheese, olives and so on; or just as it is with soups or salads. Focaccia reheats well too – just wrap it in foil and pop it into a really hot oven for about 10 minutes.

1 tsp Easybake yeast
500g/1 lb 2 oz strong white bread flour
2 tsp fine sea salt
320ml/11 fl oz water
5 tbsp olive oil
Semolina
2 generous tsp freeze-dried oregano
Sea salt flakes
Extra olive oil

1. Put the yeast, flour, fine salt and water into the bread pan in the correct order for your machine. Add 2 tbsp oil.

2. Fit the pan into the bread machine and close the lid.

3. Select the PIZZA or WHITE DOUGH setting and the SIZE if appropriate. Press Start.

4. When the program has finished, turn the dough on to a lightly floured surface and knead, knocking out the air, until smooth and elastic.

5. Using a rolling pin or your hands, roll or push the dough out into a rough oval or rectangular shape (this will need patience and perseverance because the dough will keep shrinking back again) about 1.5cm/½ in thick (no need to be too fussy though).

6. Dust a baking tray with semolina and place the dough on top. Drizzle the remaining 3 tbsp oil as evenly as you can over the top and sprinkle with the oregano. Using your fingers on one hand, make lots of deep indents all over the dough.

7. Leave to rise in a warm place until the dough has doubled in height. There is no need to cover it as the oil keeps it moist.

8. Put into a hot oven at 220°C (Fan 200°C), 425°F, Gas 7 and bake for about 15 minutes until golden brown and cooked through.

9. Take the bread out of the oven, generously drizzle extra olive oil over the top and sprinkle with a light covering of sea salt flakes.

10. Leave to cool on a wire rack.

Focaccia with Olives and Rosemary

Follow the recipe above, omitting the oregano. Scatter a handful of roughly chopped olives and some chopped fresh rosemary over the dough (before adding the oil) in step 6.

Middle Eastern Flatbreads

Should be crisp and dry on the bottom, and soft and slightly chewy on top; tear off pieces to reveal the warm air pockets between. Best served warm, straight from the oven. If made in advance, sprinkle lightly with water and pop into a hot oven to reheat for a couple of minutes only.

Makes 8

1 tsp Easybake yeast
500g/1 lb 2 oz strong white bread flour
1½ tsp fine sea salt
300ml/½ pt water
2 tbsp olive oil
Beaten egg
Seeds such as sesame, nigella, poppy, or a mixture

1. Put all the ingredients, except the egg and seeds, into the bread pan in the correct order for your machine. Fit the pan into the bread machine and close the lid.

2. Select the WHITE DOUGH setting and the SIZE if appropriate. Press Start.

3. Meanwhile, remove the oven shelves (to prevent burns as you lean into the hot oven) and put a large baking tray on the bottom or the bottom shelf. Preheat to 240°C (Fan 220°C), 475°F, Gas 9. (A fan oven produced the best results for me.)

4. When the program has finished, turn the dough on to a lightly floured surface and knead, knocking out the air, until smooth and elastic.

5. Divide the mixture into eight equal pieces and shape each one into a ball. Place on the floured surface, cover with a dry cloth and leave to rest for 10 minutes (to make rolling out easier).

6. With a rolling pin, roll one piece of dough out thinly until it measures about 20cm/8 in. Repeat with the second piece. Brush their tops with beaten egg and sprinkle some seeds over.

7. Transfer them to the hot baking tray in the oven and bake for 3-5 minutes until puffed up, cooked and just beginning to colour around the edges. Meanwhile, roll out the next two.

8. Remove from the oven and wrap gently in a dry cloth, adding the others as they come out of the oven.

Pitta Bread

*Probably the best known of the Middle Eastern flatbreads,
pitta bread is pale and soft. When split, it has a natural pocket
that's ideal for filling with salad, vegetables, meat, kebabs or
falafel – ideal for packed lunches and outdoor eating. Serve it
too with meze or dips, such as hummus or taramasalata.*

Makes 12

1 tsp Easybake yeast
500g/1 lb 2 oz strong white bread flour
1 tsp fine sea salt
300ml/½ pt water
1 tbsp olive oil

1. Put all the ingredients into the bread pan in the correct
    order for your machine. Fit the pan into the bread
    machine and close the lid.
2. Select the WHITE DOUGH setting and the SIZE if
    appropriate. Press Start.
3. When the program has finished, turn the dough on to a
    lightly floured surface and knead lightly, knocking out
    the air.
4. Divide the mixture into 12 equal pieces and shape each
    one into a ball. Place on the floured surface, cover with
    a dry cloth and leave to rest for 10 minutes (to make
    rolling out easier).
5. With a floured rolling pin, roll out each ball into an oval
    or circle about 15cm/6 in wide and 0.5cm/¼ in thick.
    Place on the floured surface, cover with the cloth and
    leave to rise for 20-30 minutes.
6. Meanwhile, put two or three baking trays in the oven
    and preheat to 240°C (Fan 220°C), 475°F, Gas 9. (A fan
    oven produced the best results for me.)
7. Transfer some of the dough pieces on to one hot
    baking tray. Bake for about 3 minutes or until puffed up
    and cooked, but not browned.
8. Take them out of the oven and leave on a wire rack to
    cool slightly before covering with a dry cloth (to keep
    the crust soft) and leaving to cool.
9. Cook the remaining dough pieces in the same way.

Naan Bread

Probably the best known Indian flatbread, naan is traditionally made with yogurt. Serve it warm with your favourite spicy dishes. If liked, sprinkle some sesame seeds over the naan after brushing them in step 6 and before baking them in the hot oven or crush some garlic into the ghee or butter.

Makes 8

1 tsp Easybake yeast
500g/1 lb 2 oz strong white bread flour
1 tsp fine sea salt
150ml carton natural yogurt
150ml/¼ pt milk
2 tsp golden caster sugar
25g/1 oz ghee or clarified butter (plus extra melted, for
  brushing)

1. Put the ingredients into the bread pan in the correct order for your machine, adding 3 tbsp water. Fit the pan into the bread machine and close the lid.

2. Select the WHITE DOUGH setting and the SIZE if appropriate. Press Start.

3. Meanwhile preheat the oven to 230°C (Fan 210°C), 450°F, Gas 8.

4. When the program has finished, turn the dough on to a lightly floured surface and knead, knocking out the air, until smooth and elastic.

5. Divide the mixture into eight equal pieces and roll each one into an oval or teardrop shape about 23cm/9 in long. Place on the floured surface, cover with a dry cloth and leave to rise for 10 minutes only.

6. Heat one or two oiled baking sheets in the hot oven. Lay two or three naan on the hot baking sheet and quickly brush with melted ghee or butter.

7. Put into the hot oven and cook for about 10 minutes until puffed up and only just browned. Repeat with the remaining dough.

Pesto Rolls

These delightfully misshapen rolls are so easy to make and bake, either in a ring mould or in a cake tin (seven pieces around the edge and one in the centre). Once they are cooked, just invert the tin, give it a shake and the rolls come tumbling out.

Makes 8

1 tsp Easybake yeast
350g/12 oz strong white bread flour
150g/6 oz granary-style or malted grain flour
1 tsp fine sea salt
300ml/½ pt water
3 tbsp olive oil
2 tbsp pesto (from a jar)

1. Put the first five ingredients into the bread pan with 1 tbsp oil in the correct order for your machine.
2. Fit the pan into the bread machine and close the lid.
3. Select the WHITE DOUGH setting and the SIZE if appropriate. Press Start.
4. When the program has finished, turn the dough on to a lightly floured surface and knead well, knocking out the air, until smooth and elastic. With a sharp knife, cut the dough into eight roughly equal pieces.
5. Lightly brush a 24-25cm/9½-10 in ring mould with oil.
6. Put the pesto into a shallow bowl (a cereal bowl is fine) and stir in the remaining oil.
7. Put a dough piece into the mixture and, using two forks, turn it gently until coated on all sides. Still using the forks, transfer it to the mould. Repeat the process, using up the remaining dough pieces and filling the mould. Drizzle any remaining pesto mixture over the top.
8. Leave to rise in a warm place until the dough has doubled in size. There is no need to cover it.
9. Put into a hot oven at 200°C (Fan 180°C), 400°F, Gas 6 and bake for about 15-20 minutes until golden brown and cooked through.
10. Leave to stand for about 5 minutes before shaking the rolls out on to a wire rack.

Italian-style Bread

A rustic-looking loaf with an uneven texture and irregular pockets of air that is similar to, but denser than, ciabatta. Don't be alarmed at the stickiness of the dough when it comes out of the bread machine – just make sure that your fingers and baking tray are really well floured.

1 tsp Easybake yeast
500g/1 lb 2 oz strong white bread flour
1½ tsp fine sea salt
3 tbsp olive oil
350ml/12 fl oz water

1. Put the ingredients into the bread pan in the correct order for your machine.

2. Fit the pan into the bread machine and close the lid.

3. Select the WHITE DOUGH setting and the SIZE if appropriate. Press Start.

4. When the program has finished, carefully ease the very-sticky dough (I use a flexible plastic spatula) on to a large thickly-floured baking tray – trying not to knock the air out of it. Once it is on the baking tray, use well floured fingers to gently pat out into a regular shape that is about 3.5cm/1½ in thick. Dust the top surface with more flour.

5. Leave to rise, uncovered, until the dough has doubled in size.

6. Meanwhile, preheat the oven to 220°C (Fan 200°C), 425°F, Gas 7.

7. Put into the hot oven and bake for about 30 minutes until golden brown and cooked through.

8. Transfer to a wire rack and leave to cool.

Free-form Wholemeal

This is an excellent wholemeal loaf that looks rustic and tastes really nutty and delicious. Once the bread machine has made the dough, shape it by hand and leave to rise for as long as it needs to double in size. The baked loaf has a large area of delicious crust. The addition of a little oil and vinegar helps to keep the texture moist.

1½ tsp Easybake yeast
500g/1 lb 2 oz strong wholemeal flour
1¼ tsp fine sea salt
1 tsp muscovado sugar
2 tsp vinegar
350ml/12 fl oz water
1½ tbsp olive oil

1. Put the ingredients into the bread pan in the correct order for your machine. Fit the pan into the bread machine and close the lid.

2. Select the WHOLEWHEAT DOUGH setting and the SIZE if appropriate. Press Start.

3. When the program has finished, turn the dough on to a lightly floured surface and knead, knocking out the air, until smooth and elastic (the dough should feel quite soft).

4. Pat the dough into a flat circle about 23cm/9 in diameter and place on a greased baking sheet. Cover with oiled film and leave to rise until doubled in size.

5. Meanwhile preheat the oven to 190°C (Fan 170°C), 375°F, Gas 5.

6. Remove the film, put into the hot oven and cook for about 40 minutes or until golden brown and cooked through.

7. Transfer to a wire rack and leave to cool.

Challah

Here is my version of the traditional Jewish Sabbath bread. The rich dough is made with eggs, the texture is light and the crust is soft. It is most often shaped into a plait or braid. Not suitable for use with the delay timer.

1½ tsp Easybake yeast
500g/1 lb 2 oz strong white bread flour
½ tsp fine sea salt
55g/2 oz butter, cut into small pieces
2 tbsp clear honey
2 medium eggs, beaten
200ml/7 fl oz water
Beaten egg, to glaze
Poppy seeds

1. Put the first seven ingredients into the bread pan in the correct order for your machine. Fit the pan into the bread machine and close the lid.
2. Select the WHITE DOUGH setting and the SIZE if appropriate. Press Start.
3. When the program has finished, turn the dough on to a lightly floured surface and knead lightly, knocking out the air.
4. Divide the mixture into 3 equal pieces and roll each one into a sausage shape about 40cm/16 in long. Lay the strands alongside each other and pinch one set of ends together. Now plait the dough (lifting the right and left strands alternately over the middle one) and then pinch the loose ends neatly together.
5. Lift the plait on to a lightly buttered baking tray, cover with lightly oiled clear film and leave to rise at room temperature until doubled in size.
6. Meanwhile, preheat the oven to 180°C (Fan 160°C), 350°F, Gas 4.
7. Carefully remove the film and brush the risen dough with beaten egg. Top with a generous sprinkling of poppy seeds.
8. Put into the hot oven and cook for about 45 minutes until cooked through and the loaf sounds hollow when tapped underneath.
9. Transfer to a wire rack and leave to cool.

Bara Brith

Bara Brith is Welsh for 'speckled bread'. The lightly-spiced dough is made with strong tea – mostly I use ordinary breakfast tea; occasionally I add Earl Grey to give the loaf a really special flavour. Serve it cold, sliced and spread with butter.

7g sachet Easybake yeast
450g/1 lb strong white bread flour
50g/2 oz light muscovado sugar
1 tsp fine sea salt
¾ tsp ground mixed spice
50g/1¾ oz butter, cut into small pieces
350ml/12 fl oz cooled strong tea, strained
225g/8 oz mixed dried fruit – currants, raisins, sultanas
and finely chopped peel

1. Put all the ingredients except the fruit into the bread pan in the correct order for your machine. Fit the pan into the bread machine and close the lid.

2. Select the WHITE DOUGH RAISIN setting and the SIZE if appropriate. Press Start. When the machine indicates (with a beeping sound), add the fruit and close the lid again.

3. When the program has finished, turn the dough on to a lightly floured surface and knead lightly, knocking out the air, until smooth.

4. Shape the dough and place, smooth side upwards, in a lightly buttered loaf tin measuring about 23 x 12.5cm/ 9 x 5 in. (I usually line the base with baking paper too.)

5. Cover loosely with lightly oiled clear film and leave to rise at room temperature until doubled in size.

6. Meanwhile, preheat the oven to 200°C (Fan 180°C), 400°F, Gas 6.

7. Carefully remove the film, put into the hot oven and cook for about 40 minutes until cooked through and the loaf sounds hollow when tapped underneath.

8. Turn out on to a wire rack and leave to cool.

Barm Brack

A rich and spicy Irish fruit bread that is traditionally served in buttered slices. Like the Welsh Bara Brith of the previous recipe this too is sometimes made with cooled strong tea.

7g sachet Easybake yeast
450g/1 lb strong white bread flour
85g/3 oz golden caster sugar
1 tsp fine sea salt
1½ tsp ground cinnamon
85g/3 oz butter, cut into small pieces
1 medium egg, beaten
250ml/9 fl oz milk (I use semi-skimmed)
150g/5½ oz currants
25g/1 oz finely chopped peel
1 tbsp sugar mixed with 1 tbsp boiling water, to glaze

1. Put the first eight ingredients into the bread pan in the correct order for your machine. Fit the pan into the bread machine and close the lid.
2. Select the WHITE DOUGH RAISIN setting and the SIZE if appropriate. Press Start. When the machine indicates (with a beeping sound), add the currants and peel and close the lid again.
3. When the program has finished, turn the dough on to a lightly floured surface and knead lightly, knocking out the air, until smooth.
4. Shape the dough into a ball and place, smooth side upwards, in a lightly buttered 20cm/8 in cake tin. (I line the base with baking paper.)
5. Cover loosely with lightly oiled clear film and leave to rise at room temperature until doubled in size.
6. Meanwhile, preheat the oven to 200°C (Fan 180°C), 400°F, Gas 6.
7. Carefully remove the film, put into the hot oven and cook for about 40 minutes until cooked through and the loaf sounds hollow when tapped underneath.
8. Brush the top of the loaf with the glaze and return to the oven for 2-3 minutes.
9. Turn out on to a wire rack, brush with the remaining glaze and leave to cool.

Saffron Fruit Bread

Saffron, one of the world's most expensive spices, gives this traditional Cornish loaf its distinctive flavour and beautiful golden colour. I prefer to use saffron strands but you could use powder. Serve it sliced and buttered.

Good pinch of saffron strands
2 tsp Easybake yeast
450g/1 lb strong white bread flour
50g/1¾ oz golden caster sugar
1 tsp fine sea salt
50g/1¾ oz butter, cut into small pieces
50g/1¾ oz lard, cut into small pieces
150ml/¼ pt milk
55g/2 oz currants
55g/2 oz sultanas
55g/2 oz finely chopped peel
Beaten egg, to glaze

1. Put the saffron into a bowl, pour over 150ml/¼ pt boiling water, cover and leave to stand for at least 3-4 hours (or overnight if you like) to allow the colour and flavour to develop.

2. Put the yeast, flour, sugar, salt, butter, lard, milk and saffron mixture into the bread pan in the correct order for your machine. Fit the pan into the bread machine and close the lid.

3. Select the WHITE DOUGH RAISIN setting and the SIZE if appropriate. Press Start. When the machine indicates (with a beeping sound), add the currants, sultanas and peel and close the lid again.

4. When the program has finished, turn the dough on to a lightly floured surface and knead lightly, knocking out the air, until smooth.

5. Shape the dough and place, smooth side upwards, in a lightly buttered loaf tin measuring about 23 x 12.5cm/ 9 x 5 in. (I line the base with baking paper too.)

6. Cover loosely with lightly oiled clear film and leave to rise at room temperature until doubled in size.

7. Meanwhile, preheat the oven to 200°C (Fan 180°C), 400°F, Gas 6.

8. Carefully remove the film and brush the top with beaten egg.

9. Put into the hot oven and cook for about 40 minutes or until cooked through and the loaf sounds hollow when tapped underneath.

10. Turn out on to a wire rack and leave to cool.

Hot Cross Buns

Homemade buns are so much nicer than the pre-packed ready-made varieties. Traditionally they are eaten on Good Friday though they are delicious served warm (split and buttered) or toasted at any time of the year.

Makes 12

7g sachet Easybake yeast
500g/1 lb 2 oz strong white bread flour
50g/1½ oz golden caster sugar
½ tsp fine sea salt
2½ tsp ground mixed spice
85g/3 oz butter, cut into small pieces
1 medium egg, beaten
250ml/9 fl oz milk (I use semi-skimmed)
100g/3½ oz mixed dried fruit – currants, raisins and finely chopped peel

Crosses:
50g/1½ oz plain flour

Glaze:
20g/¾ oz golden caster sugar
1 tbsp milk

1. Put all the ingredients, except the fruit, into the bread pan in the correct order for your machine. Fit the pan into the bread machine and close the lid.

2. Select the WHITE DOUGH RAISIN setting and the SIZE if appropriate. Press Start. When the machine indicates

(with a beeping sound), add the fruit and close the lid again.

3. When the program has finished, turn the dough on to a lightly floured surface and knead lightly, knocking out the air, until smooth.

4. Divide the dough into 12 pieces and shape each one into a ball. Arrange, smooth side up and about 1cm/ ½ in apart, on one or two lightly buttered baking sheet(s). Cover with oiled film and leave in a warm place for about 30 minutes or until doubled in size.

5. Meanwhile, preheat the oven to 190°C (Fan 170°C), 375°F, Gas 5.

6. Blend the flour for the crosses with about 5 tbsp cold water to make a smooth thick paste and spoon the mixture into a piping bag with a small plain nozzle (I usually make one quickly out of baking or greaseproof paper and cut the tip off with scissors).

7. Carefully remove the film and pipe a cross on to each one.

8. Put into the hot oven and cook for about 20 minutes until cooked through.

9. Meanwhile, make the glaze by dissolving the sugar in 1 tbsp boiling water. Stir in the milk.

10. Transfer the buns to a wire rack and brush with the glaze. Leave for several minutes before brushing with the glaze again. Leave to cool.

Tea Cakes

Everyone's favourite split and toasted for tea or, indeed, at any time of the day. Add a little ground mixed spice to the flour if you like.

Makes 8

1 tsp Easybake yeast
450g/1 lb strong white bread flour
1 tsp fine sea salt
2 tbsp golden caster sugar
50g/1¾ oz butter, cut into small pieces
280ml/9½ fl oz water
85g/3 oz currants
25g/1 oz finely chopped mixed peel

Glaze:
1 tbsp golden caster sugar
1 tbsp milk

1. Put the first six ingredients into the bread pan in the correct order for your machine. Fit the pan into the bread machine and close the lid.
2. Select the WHITE DOUGH RAISIN setting and the SIZE if appropriate. Press Start. When the machine indicates (with a beeping sound), add the currants and peel and close the lid again.
3. When the program has finished, turn the dough on to a lightly floured surface and knead lightly, knocking out the air, until smooth.
4. Divide the dough into eight pieces and shape each one into a ball. Arrange, smooth side up and spaced apart, on lightly buttered baking sheets. Cover with oiled film and leave until doubled in size.
5. Meanwhile, preheat the oven to 220°C (Fan 200°C), 425°F, Gas 7.
6. Remove the film, put into the hot oven and cook for about 20 minutes until cooked through.
7. Meanwhile, make the glaze by heating the sugar in the milk and stirring until dissolved (I do this in the microwave).
8. When the tea cakes are cooked, brush them with the glaze and return to the oven for 1-2 minutes.
9. Transfer to a wire rack and leave to cool.

Devonshire Splits

Also known as Cornish Splits or Chudleighs, these small round buns are sprinkled with icing sugar. They have a soft, light texture and are golden brown on top and pale towards the bottom. Serve them split and filled with jam and whipped or clotted cream. If you decide to delay the program, replace the milk with water and 2 tbsp milk powder.

Makes 14

1 tsp Easybake yeast
450g/1 lb strong white bread flour
1 tsp fine sea salt
1 tsp golden caster sugar
50g/1¾ oz butter, cut into small pieces
300ml/10 fl oz milk
Icing sugar

1. Put all the ingredients, except the icing sugar, into the bread pan in the correct order for your machine. Fit the pan into the bread machine and close the lid.

2. Select the WHITE DOUGH setting and the SIZE if appropriate. Press Start.

3. When the program has finished, turn the dough on to a lightly floured surface and knead lightly, knocking out the air, until smooth.

4. Divide the dough into 14 pieces and shape each one into a ball. Arrange them, smooth side up and about 1cm/½ in apart, on a lightly floured baking sheet. Cover with oiled film and leave until doubled in size.

5. Meanwhile, preheat the oven to 220°C (Fan 200°C), 425°F, Gas 7.

6. Remove the film, put into the hot oven and cook for 15-20 minutes until golden on top and cooked through.

7. Transfer to a wire rack, sift over some icing sugar and leave to cool.

Sally Lunn

These small round loaves are a speciality of the spa town of Bath. They have a shiny dark-golden crust on top and a rich crumb that is close-textured and light. Traditionally the warm buns are split horizontally once or twice, spread with butter or thick cream, re-assembled and eaten straight away. This recipe is not suitable for delayed programs.

Makes 2

2 medium eggs
Milk
1 tsp Easybake yeast
450g/1 lb strong white bread flour
1 tsp fine sea salt
1 tsp golden caster sugar
50g/1¾ oz butter, cut into small pieces
2 tsp finely grated lemon rind

Glaze:
1 tbsp golden caster sugar
1 tbsp milk

1. Lightly beat the eggs and make up to 300ml/½ pt with milk.
2. Put all the ingredients, including the egg mixture into the bread pan in the correct order for your machine. Fit the pan into the bread machine and close the lid.
3. Select the WHITE DOUGH setting and the SIZE if appropriate. Press Start.
4. When the program has finished, turn the dough on to a lightly floured surface and knead lightly, knocking out the air, until smooth.
5. Divide the dough into two pieces and shape each one into a ball. Place them, smooth side up, into two lightly buttered 15cm/6 in cake tins. Cover with oiled film and leave until doubled in size.
6. Meanwhile, preheat the oven to 220°C (Fan 200°C), 425°F, Gas 7.
7. Remove the film, put into the hot oven and cook for 15-20 minutes until dark golden on top and cooked through.
8. Meanwhile, make the glaze by heating the sugar in the milk and stirring until dissolved (I do this in the micro-wave).
9. Transfer to a wire rack and while the loaves are still hot, brush the tops with the glaze.

Chelsea Buns

Best served warm, these loose spiral buns are sometimes topped with thin icing made with icing sugar and water, though I usually use a glaze of sugar and milk. This recipe is not suitable for delayed programs.

Makes 18

1 tsp Easybake yeast
450g/1 lb strong white bread flour
1 tsp fine sea salt
25g/1 oz butter or lard, cut into small pieces
2 eggs, beaten
200ml/7 fl oz milk
85g/3 oz currants
2 tbsp finely chopped mixed peel
50g/1¾ oz light muscovado sugar
1 tsp ground mixed spice
Melted butter

Glaze:
1 tbsp golden caster sugar
1 tbsp milk

1. Put the first six ingredients into the bread pan in the correct order for your machine. Fit the pan into the bread machine and close the lid.

2. Select the WHITE DOUGH setting and the SIZE if appropriate. Press Start.

3. When the program has finished, turn the dough on to a lightly floured surface and knead lightly, knocking out the air, until smooth.

4. Keeping the surface lightly floured, roll out the dough into a rectangle measuring about 55 x 23cm/22 x 9 in (it may be easier to cut the dough into two equal pieces and roll out two rectangles, each measuring about 27.5 x 23cm/11 x 9 in).

5. Mix the currants with the peel, sugar and spice. Brush the dough with melted butter and scatter the fruit mixture over the top. Roll up from a long side, Swiss-roll fashion. Slice into 18 equal pieces and arrange, cut side

down, in two lightly buttered 17.5cm/7 in square cake tins (nine in each).

6. Cover with oiled film and leave to rise until the sides of the rolls are touching and the dough feels springy.

7. Meanwhile, preheat the oven to 200°C (Fan 180°C), 400°F, Gas 6.

8. Remove the film, put into the hot oven and cook for 15-20 minutes until golden brown and cooked through.

9. Meanwhile, make the glaze by heating the sugar in the milk and stirring until dissolved (I do this in the microwave).

10. When the buns are cooked, brush the tops with the glaze. To serve, gently tear the buns apart.

Panettone

Here is the famous Italian Christmas bread. It's worth buying and finely chopping large pieces of candied peel for this (rather than ready-prepared chopped dried peel) – the flavour will be much more authentic, and nicer too. The fruit is mixed into the dough when it comes out of the bread machine. Serve it like cake, cut into slices or wedges.

1½ tsp Easybake yeast
400g/14 oz strong white bread flour
50g/1¾ oz golden caster sugar
1 tsp fine sea salt
Finely grated rind of 1 lemon
115g/4 oz unsalted butter, melted
150ml/¼ pt milk
3 medium egg yolks
1 tsp vanilla extract
85g/3 oz finely chopped candied peel
55g/2 oz raisins
1 egg yolk, to glaze

1. Put the first nine ingredients into the bread pan in the correct order for your machine. Fit the pan into the bread machine and close the lid.

2.   Select the WHITE DOUGH setting and the SIZE if appropriate. Press Start.

3.   Meanwhile, butter a 15cm/6 in round cake tin. Line the base with a circle of baking paper. Cut a strip of baking paper about 12.5cm/5 in wide and use it to line the sides (so that it stands proud of the tin).

4.   When the program has finished, turn the dough on to a lightly floured surface and knead lightly, knocking out the air, until smooth.

5.   Add the peel and raisins, kneading until well combined.

6.   Shape the dough into a ball and place in the prepared tin.

7.   Lay a piece of clear film on top of the paper to cover and leave to rise in a warm room temperature until the centre of the dough just reaches the top of the paper.

8.   Meanwhile, preheat the oven to 200°C (Fan 180°C), 400°F, Gas 6. Make the glaze by beating the egg yolk with about 1 tsp cold water.

9.   Remove the film and carefully brush the top of the dough with the egg-yolk glaze. With a very sharp knife, cut a shallow cross in the top.

10. Put into the hot oven and cook for 10 minutes, then lower the temperature to 180°C (Fan 160°C), 350°F, Gas 4 for 30-40 minutes

11. Leave to cool in the tin before turning out on to a wire rack and cooling completely. Remove the paper just before serving.

Stollen

Stollen is a traditional German Christmas cake. It's rich with butter and laden with dried fruit. Don't be put off by the long recipe because, with a bread machine, it's really quite easy. Store it in an airtight container or tightly wrapped in foil for one week before serving. By the way, the custom is to bake two – one for yourself and one to give away.

Dough:
7g packet Easybake yeast
500g/1 lb 2 oz strong white bread flour
85g/3 oz golden caster sugar
1 tsp fine sea salt
150g/5½ oz unsalted butter, cut into small pieces
150ml/¼ pt milk
2 large eggs, beaten (about 100ml/3½ fl oz in total)
1½ tsp vanilla extract

Fruit-and-nut mixture:
150g/5 oz raisins
115g/4 oz currants
115g/4 oz finely chopped candied peel
115g/4 oz blanched almonds, roughly chopped
Finely grated rind of 1 lemon
Finely grated rind of 1 orange
1 tsp ground cinnamon or cardamom
1 tsp freshly grated nutmeg
2 tbsp rum

Sugar coating:
85g/3 oz golden caster sugar
55g/2 oz icing sugar
1 tsp vanilla extract

140g/5 oz unsalted butter, melted

1. Put the dough ingredients into the bread pan in the correct order for your machine. Fit the pan into the bread machine and close the lid.

2. Select the WHITE DOUGH setting and the SIZE if appropriate. Press Start.

3. Meanwhile, combine the fruit-and-nut ingredients in a bowl and leave to stand. Put the sugars and vanilla

extract into a second bowl and rub the mixture between your fingers until well mixed and slightly crumbly.

4.   When the program has finished, turn the dough on to a lightly floured surface and knead lightly, knocking out the air, until smooth.

5.   Roll out the dough to about 2.5cm/1 in thick. Spread the fruit-and-nut mixture over the top, roll up and knead until well incorporated.

6.   Divide the dough into two equal pieces. Roll each one into an oval about 2.5cm/1 in thick and place on one or two buttered baking sheets.

7.   Use the side of your hand to make an indentation lengthways down the centre of the dough. Fold the dough over lengthways so that the top layer does not quite reach the edge of the bottom layer. Again, using the side of your hand, make a slight indentation lengthways down the centre.

8.   Cover with a tea towel and leave to rise in a warm room temperature for about 30 minutes (it needs to rise but not to double its size).

9.   Meanwhile, preheat the oven to 180°C (Fan 160°C), 350°F, Gas 4.

10. Remove cover, put into the hot oven and cook for about 45 minutes until cooked through.

11. Remove from the oven and brush all over (including the bases of the cakes) with the melted butter until it is all used up. Scatter the sugar coating all over each cake, using your hands if necessary to spread it evenly over.

12. Leave to cool completely on a wire rack.

Marzipan Stollen

Make the Stollen recipe as above. Roll 250g/9 oz marzipan into two long sausage shapes and, in step 7, lay one down the length of each piece of dough before folding it over. You will not be able to make the second indentation.

Bagels (1)

Traditional Jewish rolls, bagels are shiny doughnut-shapes with a texture that is denser than normal bread and a crust that is chewy. The secret is to make them with water, add no fat and cook the dough briefly in boiling water (I sweeten it with malt extract) before baking in a hot oven. Homemade bagels like these may not look as even and tidy as the shop-bought variety but boy do they taste good! Serve them warm or at room temperature, split with your favourite fillings added – my preference is for cream cheese, smoked salmon and chives; or thinly sliced pastrami, cheese and red onion with mayonnaise and salad leaves.

Makes 8

¾ tsp Easybake yeast
500g/1 lb 2 oz strong white bread flour
1½ tsp fine sea salt
1 tsp golden caster sugar
300ml/½ pt water
1 generous tbsp malt extract
1 egg, beaten with a pinch of salt, to glaze

1. Put the first five ingredients into the bread pan in the correct order for your machine.

2. Fit the pan into the bread machine and close the lid.

3. Select the WHITE DOUGH setting and the SIZE if appropriate. Press Start.

4. When the program has finished, turn the dough on to a lightly floured surface and knead well, knocking out the air, until very smooth and elastic.

5. Cut the dough into 8 pieces and shape each piece into a very smooth ball. Flatten the ball slightly and then push your floured finger through the centre to make a hole. Twirl the dough first round one finger, then round two, until the hole is about 5cm/2 in diameter (though this may look too large, the hole will close up slightly during cooking). Lay it on the worktop and gently ease it into a circular shape. Repeat with the remaining dough.

6. Cover with a tea towel and leave to rise for 15-20 minutes only.

7. Meanwhile, preheat the oven to 220°C (Fan 200°C), 425°F, Gas 7.

8. Pour water into a wide pan to about 5cm/2 in deep, add the malt extract and bring to a gentle boil.

9. Gently put three or four bagels into the water and cook for about 30 seconds on each side. With a slotted spoon, lift out on to kitchen paper. Repeat with the remaining bagels.

10. Arrange them on one or two lightly greased baking sheets and brush with the egg glaze.

11. Put into the hot oven and cook for 15-20 minutes until golden brown and cooked through.

12. Transfer to a wire rack and leave to cool.

Bagels (2)

These bagels, made with egg, are a richer, not-so-dense-and-chewy version of the recipe on page 108. They tend to look plumper and have a smoother finish. Serve them in a similar way, warm or at room temperature. On the rare occasions they are left to become one or two days old, we love them for breakfast – split, toasted and spread thickly with butter.

Makes 8

1 tsp Easybake yeast
500g/1 lb 2 oz strong white bread flour
1½ tsp fine sea salt
1 tsp golden caster sugar
4 tbsp oil
2 large eggs, lightly beaten
150ml/¼ pt water
1 generous tbsp malt extract
1 egg, beaten with a pinch of salt, to glaze

1. Put the first seven ingredients into the bread pan in the correct order for your machine.

2. Fit the pan into the bread machine and close the lid.

3. Select the WHITE DOUGH setting and the SIZE if appropriate. Press Start.

4. When the program has finished, turn the dough on to a lightly floured surface and knead well, knocking out the air, until smooth and elastic.

5. Cut the dough into 8 pieces and shape each piece into a very smooth ball. Flatten the ball slightly and then push your floured finger through the centre to make a hole. Twirl the dough first round one finger, then round two, until the hole is about 5cm/2 in diameter (though this may look too large, the hole will close up slightly during cooking). Lay it on the worktop and gently ease it into a circular shape. Repeat with the remaining dough.

6. Cover with a tea towel and leave to rise for 15-20 minutes only.

7. Meanwhile, preheat the oven to 220°C (Fan 200°C), 425°F, Gas 7.

8. Pour water into a wide pan to about 5cm/2 in deep, add the malt extract and bring to a gentle boil.

9. Gently put three or four bagels into the water and cook for about 30 seconds on each side. With a slotted spoon, lift out on to kitchen paper. Repeat with the remaining bagels.

10. Arrange them on one or two lightly greased baking sheets and brush with the egg glaze.

11. Put into the hot oven and cook for 15-20 minutes until golden brown and cooked through.

12. Transfer to a wire rack and leave to cool.

Crisp-crust Rolls

In this recipe, the risen dough is simmered briefly before baking in a hot oven to produce a texture that is slightly different from normal rolls. The egg white glaze produces a splintering, crisp crust that reminds me of authentic French bread fresh out of the oven, while the inside is soft and light.

Makes 10

1 tsp Easybake yeast
500g/1 lb 2 oz strong white bread flour
1½ tsp fine sea salt
1 generous tsp malt extract
1 tbsp oil
300ml/½ pt water
1 medium egg, separated

1. Put all the ingredients, except the egg white, into the bread pan in the correct order for your machine.
2. Fit the pan into the bread machine and close the lid.
3. Select the WHITE DOUGH setting and the SIZE if appropriate. Press Start.
4. When the program has finished, turn the dough on to a floured surface and knead well, knocking out the air, until very smooth and elastic.
5. Cut the dough into 10 pieces and shape into rolls, flattening each one slightly.
6. Put on a lightly oiled baking sheet, cover with oiled film and leave to rise until doubled in size.
7. Meanwhile, preheat the oven to 220°C (Fan 200°C), 425°F, Gas 7 and lightly whisk the egg white.
8. Pour water into a wide pan to about 5cm/2 in deep and bring to a gentle simmer.
9. Gently put three or four rolls into the simmering water and cook for about 1 minute, turning them over half way. With a slotted spoon, lift out on to kitchen paper. Repeat with the remaining rolls.
10. Return the rolls to the lightly greased baking sheet and brush with the egg white.
11. Put into the hot oven and cook for about 20 minutes until golden brown and cooked through.
12. Transfer to a wire rack and leave to cool.

Salted Knots

Similar to the more loosely knotted pretzel, these rolls are soft and slightly chewy with a salty crust. Before baking in the oven, they are immersed briefly in simmering water. They go well with ham and mustard.

Makes 16

1 tsp Easybake yeast
500g/1 lb 2 oz strong white bread flour
1 tsp fine sea salt
200ml/7 fl oz water
100ml/3 fl oz milk
25g/1 oz butter, cut into small pieces
1 medium egg, beaten with 1 tbsp milk, to glaze
sea salt crystals

1. Put the first six ingredients into the bread pan in the correct order for your machine.
2. Fit the pan into the bread machine and close the lid.
3. Select the WHITE DOUGH setting and the SIZE if appropriate. Press Start.
4. When the program has finished, turn the dough on to a floured surface and knead well, knocking out the air, until very smooth and elastic.
5. Cut the dough into 16 pieces and shape into balls. Cover with a tea towel and leave to rest for 5 minutes.
6. Roll each ball into a long sausage and tie loosely into a knot.
7. Put on a lightly oiled baking sheet and leave to rise for just 10-15 minutes.
8. Meanwhile, preheat the oven to 200°C (Fan 180°C), 400°F, Gas 6.
9. Bring a large pan of salted water to a gentle simmer and immerse the rolls, three or four at a time, in the water for about 30 seconds. With a slotted spoon, lift out and drain briefly on kitchen paper then return the rolls to the lightly greased baking sheet.
10. Brush with the egg glaze and sprinkle with salt crystals.
11. Put into the hot oven and cook for 20-25 minutes until golden brown and cooked through.
12. Transfer to a wire rack and leave to cool.

Cheese and Spring Onion Rolls

Children love to make these, with or without the onions. They are delicious served slightly warm while the cheese inside is still soft.

Makes 12

1 tsp Easybake yeast
500g/1 lb 2 oz strong white bread flour
1 tsp fine sea salt
1 tsp mustard powder
4 large spring onions, finely chopped
300ml/½ pt water
85g/3 oz firm cheese, such as feta or Cheddar, cut into 12 cubes
Freshly grated Parmesan cheese (optional)

1. Put all the ingredients, except for the cheeses, into the bread pan in the correct order for your machine.
2. Fit the pan into the bread machine and close the lid.
3. Select the WHITE DOUGH setting and the SIZE if appropriate. Press Start.
4. When the program has finished, turn the dough on to a lightly floured surface and knead well, knocking out the air, until smooth and elastic.
5. Cut the dough into 12 pieces and shape into balls. Push one cube of cheese into the centre of each dough ball and pinch the edges together to seal it well. Arrange, smooth side up and with plenty of space between them, on a greased baking tray.
6. Cover with oiled film and leave to rise until doubled in size.
7. Meanwhile, preheat the oven to 220°C (Fan 200°C), 425°F, Gas 7.
8. Remove the film and, if using, sprinkle the tops with a little Parmesan.
9. Put into the hot oven and cook for about 15 minutes until golden brown and cooked through.
10. Transfer to a wire rack and leave to cool.

Marmite Loaf

This one is for Marmite lovers – adjust the amount to suit your own taste. I think the best result is obtained by making the dough in the bread machine and baking the loaf in the oven. However, if you prefer to cook it in the bread machine, add an extra tablespoon of water and use the BASIC WHITE setting, LIGHT CRUST and the appropriate SIZE.

1¼ tsp Easybake yeast
500g/1 lb 2 oz strong white bread flour
1 tbsp golden caster sugar
1 tbsp oil
1 generous tbsp Marmite
325ml/11 fl oz water

1. Put the ingredients into the bread pan in the correct order for your machine.

2. Fit the pan into the bread machine and close the lid.

3. Select the WHITE DOUGH setting and the SIZE if appropriate. Press Start.

4. When the program has finished, turn the dough on to a lightly floured surface and knead, knocking out the air, until smooth and elastic.

5. Shape the dough into a large ball and place, smooth side up on a greased baking sheet. With your hand, flatten the dough slightly. Cover with oiled clear film and leave to rise at room temperature until doubled in size.

6. Meanwhile, preheat the oven to 200°C (Fan 180°C), 400°F, Gas 6.

7. Carefully remove the film. With a very sharp knife, carefully slash a shallow cross in the top of the loaf.

8. Put into the hot oven and cook for about 30 minutes until cooked through and the loaf sounds hollow when tapped underneath.

Chocolate and Pecan Loaf

This bread takes me back to camping holidays in France when the "pain van" (as my daughters used to call it) would race on to the site with its horn tooting to announce the arrival of fresh bread, croissants and pain au chocolat. We enjoy this bread for a late breakfast on the weekend, served slightly warm with mugs of freshly brewed coffee.

1 tsp Easybake yeast
500g/1 lb 2 oz strong white bread flour
½ tsp fine sea salt
1 tbsp clear honey
150ml/¼ pt milk, plus extra for brushing
150ml/¼ pt water
150g/5½ oz dark chocolate, broken into squares and roughly chopped
55g/1 oz pecans, roughly chopped

1. Put the first six ingredients into the bread pan in the correct order for your machine. Fit the pan into the bread machine and close the lid.
2. Select the WHITE DOUGH setting and the SIZE if appropriate. Press Start.
3. When the program has finished, turn the dough on to a lightly floured surface and knead well, knocking out the air until smooth and elastic.
4. Divide the mixture into two equal pieces and roll each one into a rectangle about 40cm/16 in long. Scatter the chocolate and pecans over them and roll up each piece from a long side to make two strands. Pinch the ends together then twist the strands loosely to make a thick rope.
5. Lift the loaf on to a lightly buttered baking sheet, cover with lightly oiled clear film and leave to rise at room temperature until doubled in size.
6. Meanwhile, preheat the oven to 200°C (Fan 180°C), 400°F, Gas 6.
7. Carefully remove the film and brush the risen dough with milk.
8. Put into the hot oven and cook for about 45 minutes until cooked through and the loaf sounds hollow when tapped underneath.
9. Transfer to a wire rack and leave to cool.

Croissants

If you have never had a homemade croissant, I urge you to make some this weekend! They are somewhat time-consuming but well worth the effort. Serve them warm just as they are or with good fruit-filled jam.

Makes 12

1 tsp Easybake yeast
500g/1 lb 2 oz strong white bread flour
1 tsp fine sea salt
2 tsp golden caster sugar
1 large egg, beaten
300ml/½ pt water
25g/1 oz butter
250g/9 oz unsalted butter
1 egg yolk mixed with 1 tbsp water, to glaze

1. Put the first seven ingredients into the bread pan in the correct order for your machine. Fit the pan into the bread machine and close the lid.

2. Select the WHITE DOUGH setting and the SIZE if appropriate. Press Start.

3. Meanwhile, soften the block of butter by putting it on a plate and 'mashing' it with a fork. Using the fork, divide it into three roughly-equal portions.

4. When the program has finished, turn the dough on to a lightly floured surface and knead lightly, knocking out the air, until smooth.

5. Roll out the dough into a large rectangle. With a short edge toward you, dot one-third of the butter over the top two thirds of the dough. Fold the bottom third up over the butter and the top third down. Press the rolling pin along the edges to seal them.

6. Turn the dough so that the folded edge is to the side and repeat the rolling, dotting and sealing twice more until the butter has been used up.

7. Wrap the dough in clear film and refrigerate for 20-30 minutes.

8. Repeat the rolling, folding and sealing three more times.

9. Wrap and refrigerate for 30 minutes.

10. On a lightly floured surface, roll out the dough to a rectangle measuring about 25 x 37.5cm/10 x 15 in. Cut it into six squares then cut each square diagonally into two triangles. Roll up each triangle loosely from the long edge and curve into a crescent shape.

11. Arrange, spaced well apart on one or two lightly greased baking sheets. Cover with oiled clear film and leave to rise until almost doubled in size.

12. Meanwhile, preheat the oven to 220°C (Fan 200°C), 425°F, Gas 7.

13. Carefully remove the film and brush lightly with the egg glaze.

14. Put into the hot oven and cook for 12-15 minutes until crisp and golden.

Ham and Cheese Croissants

Savoury croissants are delicious too – for breakfast or as a snack or light lunch.

Follow the recipe for Croissants, adding a thin slice each of ham and Emmenthal or Gruyère cheese before rolling up the dough triangles in step 10.

Fresh Fruit Tart

This is good made with all sorts of fruit – plums, rhubarb, gooseberries, apricots, blackberries and so on. Serve it warm for dessert with whipped cream or Greek yogurt. Chunks of it in the picnic hamper or in packed lunches should satisfy even the healthiest of appetites

1 tsp Easybake yeast
450g/1 lb strong white bread flour
1 tsp salt
2 tsp golden caster sugar
40g/1½ oz butter, cut into small pieces
250ml/9 fl oz milk

Topping:
1kg/2 lb 4 oz fresh fruit, such as plums or apricots
  (halved and stones removed)
115g/4 oz golden caster sugar

1. Put the ingredients into the bread pan in the correct order for your machine. Fit the pan into the bread machine and close the lid.
2. Select the PIZZA, QUICK DOUGH or WHITE DOUGH setting and the SIZE if appropriate. Press Start.
3. When the program has finished, turn the dough on to a lightly floured surface and knead, knocking out the air, until smooth and elastic.
4. Using a rolling pin or your hands, roll or push the dough out into a square measuring about 38cm/15 in (this will need patience and perseverance because the dough will keep shrinking back again – if it does, just allow it to relax for 5 minutes before trying again). Pinch up the sides of the dough to make a thicker edge.
5. Arrange the fruit on the dough, packing it on tightly, cut side up and leaving the thick edges free. Sprinkle with the sugar.
6. Leave to rise for 20-30 minutes only. No need to cover.
7. Meanwhile, preheat the oven to 200°C (Fan 180°C), 400°F, Gas 6.
8. Put into the hot oven and cook for about 25-30 minutes until the edges are puffed up, crisp and golden, the fruit is soft and the base is cooked through.

Kugelhopf

On a recent trip to Strasbourg, you would have found us popping into almost every boulangerie and patisserie in an attempt to find the best version of this traditional fluted celebration cake. To make it, you will need a 23cm/9 in fluted mould with a funnel up the centre – mine is metal; if yours is earthenware, add about 10 minutes to the cooking time. Serve the cake cooled on the day it is made, when it will have a wonderfully crisp crust and a soft buttery interior, or keep it for a day or two and serve it, as in the Alsace, when it will become a little drier with a good cup of coffee.

1½ tsp Easybake yeast
500g/1 lb 2 oz strong white bread flour
85g/3 oz golden caster sugar
¾ tsp fine sea salt
Finely grated rind of 1 lemon
150g/5½ oz unsalted butter, cut into small pieces
150ml/¼ pt milk
Few drops of almond extract
3 large eggs, beaten
Melted butter for brushing
About 55g/2 oz whole almonds, skin on
55g/2 oz sultanas
55g/2 oz raisins

1. Put the first nine ingredients into the bread pan in the correct order for your machine. Fit the pan into the bread machine and close the lid.

2. Select the WHITE DOUGH setting and the SIZE if appropriate. Press Start.

3. Meanwhile, brush the mould with melted butter and press the almonds into the flutes and around the sides.

4. When the program has finished, turn the dough on to a lightly floured surface and knead lightly, knocking out the air, until smooth.

5. Add the sultanas and raisins, kneading until well combined.

6. Shape the dough into a ring and carefully place in the mould.

7. Cover with a damp tea towel and leave to rise in a warm room temperature until it rises to 2.5cm/1 in below the top of the mould.

8. Meanwhile, preheat the oven to 200°C (Fan 180°C), 400°F, Gas 6.

9. Uncover, put into the hot oven and cook for about 40 minutes until golden brown and a fine skewer inserted in the centre comes out clean.

10. Leave to cool in the mould for 5 minutes before turning out on to a wire rack and cooling completely.

8

HOW DID IT TURN OUT?

Here are some of the most common results with possible explanations. When attempting to rectify a problem, make adjustments in small quantities – adding or reducing ¼ tsp yeast, ½ tsp salt, 1-2 tbsp flour, or 1-2 tbsp liquid.

Bread has not risen sufficiently:
- Not enough yeast or the yeast is stale (past its use by date or has been open to the air too long).
- Flour was poor quality or stale.
- The program used was not appropriate – too short and did not allow sufficient time for the bread to rise; or wholemeal flour was used on a white program.
- Strong bread flour was not used or too much low-gluten flour (such as buckwheat, rye, semolina or soy).
- Yeast and salt came into contact before mixing began.
- Too much salt was added (see page 20). Added ingredients can be salty, such as some cheeses.
- Ingredients were too cold (and slowed down the action of the yeast) or too hot (and the yeast was killed too early).
- Insufficient liquid made the mixture dry and heavy.
- The bread machine was opened too often or for too long during the cycle.

Uneven or misshapen top to the loaf:
- For me, an irregular finish to a loaf is not a problem. It just adds to the appeal and looks exactly what it is – homemade bread! It could, however, be due to insufficient liquid producing a dough that was too stiff.

Lots of bubbles or holes in the bread:
- Too much liquid was added.
- The dough became too warm during rising – maybe the

water was too hot when it was added or the room was extra warm.

Dough has risen too high in the bread machine (hitting the lid):
- Quantity of dough is too large for the bread machine.
- Too much yeast was added.
- The mixture was too moist.
- No salt was added or a salt substitute was used (see page 20).

Loaf rose well then collapsed during cooking:
- Too much liquid was included.
- Too much yeast was added.
- Flour quality was poor and not strong enough to support the dough.
- The program used was too long.
- No salt was added or a salt substitute was used (see page 20).
- The dough became too warm during rising – maybe the water was too hot when it was added or the room was extra warm.
- The bread machine was jolted or was sitting in a draught during cooking.

Loaf is pale:
- Adjustments may be needed to improve the colour – add a little sugar, milk or butter to promote browning or set the crust colour to dark.
- The power may have been interrupted, causing the bread machine to cool down during cooking.

Top crust is very dark or burnt:
- The dough contains too high a proportion of sugar for cooking in the bread machine – it may be preferable to make it on a DOUGH program then shape by hand before rising and baking in the oven.
- The crust colour selected was too dark.

Crust is damp or soft and wrinkled:
- The bread has been allowed to stand in the bread machine for too long after cooking, so that moisture has condensed on the top.

The sides of the loaf have collapsed:
- It has been left in the bread machine for too long after cooking.

Texture of the bread is dry:
- The mixture was dry (maybe because it contained ingredients that absorb a large amount of liquid, such as wholemeal flour or oatmeal) – next time, add a little extra liquid.

Bread is too soft (or not baked) in the centre:
- The quantity of dough was too large for the bread machine.
- The dough was too rich with too high a proportion of sugar, fat, eggs or dried fruit.
- The dough became too cold during rising – maybe the bread machine was situated in a draught.

Loose flour has stuck to the bottom and sides of the loaf:
- Ingredients may have been added to the bread pan in the wrong order, resulting in incorrect mixing.
- Too much flour was added.
- There was not enough liquid in the mixture.

Bread has mixed but has not baked:
- A DOUGH program was selected.
- A power cut has resulted in the bread machine switching off.

Extra ingredients have been mashed up into the dough instead of staying whole:
- They were added too early in the program cycle.

Extra ingredients have not been mixed in:
- They were added too late in the program cycle.

Ingredients have cooked without having been mixed:
- The kneading blade was not inserted properly or maybe not at all.

There is a smell of burning when the bread is cooking:
- Ingredients have been spilled on the heating elements.

INDEX